"What Anyone Can Do is engaging, enjoyable, and just plain fun to read. With the well-honed skills of a master storyteller, Leo Bottary shares delightful tales and practical takeaways from scores of engaging conversations with fascinating people around the central theme of supporting and learning from each other. His style is over-a-cup-of-coffee casual, but the lessons he conveys are vital to your success in work and in life. I found it immensely valuable, and you will, too."

– Jim Kouzes
Coauthor of The Leadership Challenge; *Dean's Executive Fellow of Leadership, Leavey School of Business, Santa Clara University*

"Leo makes a clear case for something many people understand intuitively, but don't always practice. You will do better in life and be more successful if you don't try and do it alone. His anecdotes, advice and wisdom are worth the read."

– JJ Ramberg
Host of Your Business *(MSNBC) and Business Owner*

"Our wealth is in our brains and our networks, but few of us know how to tap the second. Leo's new book advances the narrative of his previous excellent book, *The Power of Peers*, by embracing the full range of people who surround us. He makes a powerful case that our happiness and success can be found among those who we invite into our circle. Enlisting the support of others to help us realize our dreams is something anyone can do. This fine book shows you how."

– Rich Karlgaard
Publisher and Futurist, Forbes Media

"Leo has brought clarity and inspiration to the subject of connection within corporate structures. There has never been a more imperative time than today for us to become proactive around the necessity of teams built with healthy bones, empathy, trust, and resilience. This is elaborated upon by way of interviews and real-life scenarios that will help managers and senior executives take brave steps forward to further bring connection to their teams. I see myself sharing this book throughout our agency."

– Claude Silver
Chief Heart Officer, VaynerMedia

"If you want to make better decisions in life, surround yourself with good people. It's never too late. Leo's in my circle. You'd be wise to add him to yours too."

– @BrianSolis
Digital anthropologist, Futurist, Author of X: The Experience

"What Anyone Can Do is a brilliant primer on what we can all do as leaders to surround ourselves with a strategic network of peers who will challenge our ideas, drive us to be more disciplined, and share in our success. For all of those committed to continuous self improvement, you will find that Leo has built a step by step guide to turn aspirations into actions."

– Sam Reese
CEO, Vistage Worldwide

"Today, the smartest person in the room IS the room. Few people understand that more than Leo Bottary. This book is your step by step guide to embracing the greatest untapped and most underutilized resource we have has individuals and organizations for reaching our goals; each other."

– Angela Maiers
Founder, Choose2Matter

"We each live a human life in which we impact and are impacted by others. Leo's passion and this excellent book provide us the mindset and tools to live more fully."

– Scott Mordell
CEO of YPO

"I must say...Leo Bottary's new book, What Anyone Can Do, is one full of golden wisdom preserved for us and the generations to come. The book is right on target when explaining why some individuals make quantum leaps in their life while others are just scared to leap. It breaks down why surrounding yourself with the right people is not only important but a gift that you MUST unwrap. Make a decision and read this book because that is definitely a great action step that Any One Can Do! Keep bringing the fire Leo!"

– Rahfeal Gordon
Global Leadership Advisor + Entrepreneur

"While everyone around us is trying to build a career, a fortune, a reputation and so on, Leo Bottary is busy building people. In the end, it's all about people and no one knows that better than Leo. If you find yourself endlessly fascinating (as I find myself), you want to know how Leo sees it."

– Lewis Schiff
Chairman, Birthing of Giants

"Human beings have formed communities of practice to address shared challenges since the beginning of history. They are at the heart of what makes us human. These learning partnerships among peers have been the key to our success as a species. And in very concrete and personal ways, Leo Bottary reminds us that they are how we create our future."

– **Etienne and Beverly Wenger-Trayner**
Authors of Learning in Landscapes of Practice

"People look for answers to life's problems in the self-help aisle, but they should grab this book instead. Leo's take on teamwork stands out. Whatever your personal and professional goals, he shares a simple truth: it's the people around you who will help you get there. Leo has laid out a step by step "people plan" for individuals and teams that shows exactly how leveraging and supporting a strategic network will get you through the worst of times and will lead to the best of times. An approachable and entertaining read, it's one that you will need to buy multiple copies of. One for you, and some for the friends who surround you."

– **Ryan Foland**
Managing Partner, Influence Tree

"Success requires discipline…and a village. In order to be successful in business, you have to do things that other people won't do and do them continuously. Leo's book challenges readers to take a hard look at themselves to see what they're willing to do to be disciplined enough to reach the next level."

– **Jeffrey Hayzlett**
Primetime TV & Radio Host, Speaker, Author and Part-Time Cowboy

"My story about starting my business is very similar to Bottary's—especially the immaturity and defiance part. The only difference between our two stories is that I found Vistage before I ran out of cash and my group kicked my financial butt into gear. Without them, my story would have ended much the same. What Anyone Can Do is a breath of fresh air about the need for a coach, accountability partner, or peer group. If there is a goal we want to achieve, it has to involve some sort of help and Bottary details who you should include in your network. This book will be the holiday gift for all of our clients and every one of my friends who owns a business."

– **Gini Dietrich**
CEO of Arment Dietrich and Founder and Author of Spin Sucks

"There is no one more qualified than Leo to bring the world a little closer together. This book is a must read for everyone who wants to acquire the ninja skills needed to build a bulletproof network in business and life."

– **Brian Mac Mahon**
Sensei, Expert DOJO

"Leo drives home, with overwhelming evidence, how anything can be accomplished with a vision and a group of people to support you along that journey. I'm reminded of the poet John Dunn's famous words: no person is an island unto themselves." Those who pretend to be island need to wake up, read this book and start to harness the power of diverse expertise and accountability that peer boards maximize. You can do anything and peers are a crucial ingredient to success."

– Peter C. Fuller
President, LiveFused and Vistage Chair

"How often have you thought of yourself as 'the only one' who is experiencing both the good and the bad? How often have you suddenly found comfort, solace and a new lease on life by looking around at the people who surround you? We have made choices about those with whom we work, play, socialize and love. Leo Bottary's book, *What Anyone Can Do* is a comforting hand, a pat on the shoulder and an absolute command that we pay attention to those that surround us and step out of our isolationism. It is a reminder of Mick Jagger's comment, 'You can't always get what you want, but if you try sometimes, you might find, you get what you need.'"

– Cecelia K. Houser, Ed.D.
Principal, Korn Ferry/Hay Group

What Anyone Can Do

How Surrounding Yourself with the
Right People Will Drive Change,
Opportunity, and Personal Growth

What Anyone Can Do

How Surrounding Yourself with the Right People Will Drive Change, Opportunity, and Personal Growth

By

Leo Bottary

First edition published in 2019
by Bibliomotion, Inc.
52 Vanderbilt Avenue, New York, NY 10017, USA
2 Park Square, Milton Park, Abingdon, Oxon OX14 4RN, UK

© 2019 by Leo Bottary
Bibliomotion is an imprint of Taylor & Francis Group, an Informa business

No claim to original U.S. Government works

Printed on acid-free paper
Printed and bound by CPI Group (UK) Ltd, Croydon CR0 4YY

International Standard Book Number-13: 978-1-138-55820-5 (Hardback)
International Standard Book Number-13: 978-1-315-15129-8 (eBook)

Library of Congress Cataloging- in- Publication Data
Names: Bottary, Leo, author.
Title: What anyone can do : how surrounding yourself with the right people will drive change, opportunity, and personal growth / Leo Bottary.
Description: New York, NY : Taylor & Francis, [2018] | Includes bibliographical references and index.
Identifiers: LCCN 2018020489 (print) | LCCN 2018025340 (ebook) | ISBN 9781315151298 (e-Book) | ISBN 9781138558205 (hardback : alk. paper)
Subjects: LCSH: Business networks. | Employee motivation. | Teams in the workplace. | Leadership.
Classification: LCC HD69.S8 (ebook) | LCC HD69.S8 B684 2018 (print) | DDC 658.4/09--dc23
LC record available at https://lccn.loc.gov/2018020489

Visit the Taylor & Francis Web site at
http://www.taylorandfrancis.com

For my daughters, Kristin and Taylor, who encourage me and everyone around them to be their best selves.

There is an incredible power that comes from surrounding yourself with communities in which you feel small among them, and they look at you like a giant.

—Sekou Andrews, Poetic Voice

Contents

Foreword

If you don't go to somebody's funeral, they won't come to yours.

—Yogi Berra

The issues Leo Bottary explores in these pages have been central to shaping both my personal and my professional life. When I was thirty years old I became CEO of a startup called M5 Networks, a company that would eventually grow to employ more than 200 people. The job was a dream come true for me, but I lived in fear that our board would replace me with someone more experienced as the company became increasingly successful. I was keenly aware that, as the person in charge, my company would only grow as fast as I did. So, I set off on a path of personal development. I read books, hired coaches, brought in consultants, and took courses. But none of these things helped me develop in the job more than joining a circle of peer CEOs.

In 2008, I faced one of the toughest challenges of my life. My dad was diagnosed with a terminal illness. Simultaneously, the economy crashed. I found myself responsible for the livelihoods of my employees, the trust of my customers, and the welfare of my family, all as I dealt with this personal struggle in the background. This is not a case study that business schools teach. Throughout it all, my peer group became my backbone. With honesty and vulnerability, they helped me navigate this difficult period and uncover what it meant to lead.

I went on to sell M5, but peer circles have remained central to my life. I am an active member of three different peer groups: the Entrepreneurs' Organization (EO), Young Presidents' Organization (YPO), and the Henry Crown Fellowship. Now, as I move on to the next stage in my life, I have started Circles to try to bring the power of peer support to everyone.

Robert Putnam, in his seminal work *Bowling Alone*,[1] documented, "Without at first noticing, we've been pulled apart from our communities and each other over the last third of the century." Technological innovations over the past ten years have compounded this problem. The Internet is tricking us in two ways. First, we're connected to more people, but these connections tend to be shallow. Many find it easier to feel satisfaction by ranking up friends and likes, yet it is harder to look up from the screen into someone's eyes. This tendency is playing out at work, too. Information systems allow us to manage increasingly large and complex hierarchies of people. Video and physical conference rooms are stuffed with collaborators. But people are multitasking, distracted, and recoiling during meetings instead of capturing the magic of being a team. We have never been more connected, yet we have never acted more alone.

Second, more information does not mean more knowledge. Daily, we confront a tsunami of content. Facing our inboxes is like being stuck in a never-ending game of Space Invaders. Updates about our cat's funny dance somehow seem worth pushing to thousands of friends. We're marketing to each other, rarely conversing. Our educational system is changing slowly from an industrial and individualistic model, and gaps are widening between the workforce's skills and the way we need to work.

Much has been written about how these changes show up in the political and economic divides we see play out in the news. But it is harder to put our finger on how the changes impact our homes and offices. There's some data. Writing in 2014, political commentator David Brooks summarized two studies that showed that American adults reported an average of three close friends in 1985 but only two by 2004. According to the Conference Board, only 52.3% of Americans now like their jobs, down from 61.1% thirty years ago.

The good news is that a few leaders are pouring energy into reversing these trends. *What Anyone Can Do* is a great first step toward change. Leo Bottary has collected stories of people rejecting the John Wayne go-it-alone approach, taking off their masks, and opening up to one another. They are reclaiming the power of conversation. He's busting the "lone ranger" myth and shining a light on the personal and professional teams behind these everyday success stories. He's documenting the stark difference between traditional classrooms that line students up in rows and environments in which structured conversations with peers lead to deep learning. And he's collected in one place the best practices that make it easy for anyone to reap the rewards of this approach to work and life.

I hope that, by the end of this book, you'll ask yourself the same question I have been asking with Circles: "Why doesn't everyone have a peer group?" This question could not only have a profound impact for you on a personal level, it could fundamentally shift the way we all work with and learn from one another.

Dan Hoffman
Founder and CEO
Circles
New York, NY

Reference

1. Putnam, Robert D. *Bowling Alone: The Collapse and Revival of American Community*. New York, NY: Simon & Schuster, 2007, p. 27.

Acknowledgments

I asked guests on my *Year of the Peer* podcast to talk about the people who made a difference in their lives. Their answers included everyone from parents, friends, and co-workers to teachers, supervisors, and spouses—the kind of individuals with whom we surround ourselves each and every day. Some responses even involved people my guests had met on an airplane, whom they would never see again but who—despite a brief, finite interaction—left a positive and profound mark.

No respondents claimed to have achieved any measure of their success or happiness all on their own. Their achievements always involved a lot of people—too many to name or even remember on the spur of the moment. Many of my guests apologized preemptively for the people they knew they would forget to mention when I posed the question. Let me just say in advance that I'll do my best to recognize the wonderful people who contributed to writing *What Anyone Can Do*.

Author Robert H. Thompson suggested that I write this particular book, which is based largely on what I learned from my podcast guests, workshop participants, and peer group leaders and members during the *Year of the Peer*. While without Robert's urging, there would be no book, the *Year of the Peer* podcast was Randy Cantrell's brainchild; and no podcast, no book—at least, not this book. Randy produced the podcast and played a key role in expanding the conversation, broadening the topic from the power of peer groups to encompass the cadre of people who can make a big difference in our success and happiness if only we invite them to do so. Of course, keynote speaker and communication guru Ryan Foland served as a podcast guest, offered valuable input for framing the rationale for *Year of the Peer*, and crafted the illustrations that bring added life to each chapter. If a picture is worth a thousand words, Ryan's cartoons are worth that and then some.

No author, at least not this one, isn't helped enormously by good editors. So a big thanks to Susan Lauzau, who also edited *The Power of Peers*. I'd also like to offer a nod to Heather Pemberton Levy, who was not involved in editing this book directly, but whose advice to lead with story was in my head the entire time.

I am more grateful than I can possibly communicate to the incredible people who agreed to be my guests in 2017 on the *Year of the Peer*. Here they are, in the order they appeared on the show: Charlene Li, CEO of the Altimeter Group and Best-Selling Author; Rich Karlgaard, Publisher and Global Futurist for Forbes; Lewis Schiff, Founder and Executive Director, The Business Owners Council; JJ Ramberg, Host of Your Business (MSNBC) and Business Owner; Jim Kouzes, Co-Author of *The Leadership Challenge* (6th edition, Wiley, 2017) and former CEO; Vitaly Golomb, Investor and Global Startup Evangelist, HP Tech Ventures; Rahfeal Gordon, Inspirational Speaker/Author; Etienne and Beverly Wenger-Trayner, Scholars/Authors/Consultants; Laura Goodrich, Co-Founder, GWT Next and Author of *Seeing Red Cars* (Berrett-Kohler, 2011); Linda Darling-Hammond, Professor Emeritus, Stanford Graduate School of Education; Leon Shapiro, Co-Author of *The Power of Peers* (Bibliomotion, 2016) and former CEO of Vistage; Bri Seeley and Thais Sky, leadership and life coaches; Lolly Daskal, Founder, Lead From Within; Pat Wadors, former CHRO LinkedIn, CHRO ServiceNow; Larry Robertson, Founder Lighthouse Consulting; Sekou Andrews, Poetic Voice; Paul Michelman, MIT Sloan Management Review; Marian Salzman, CEO Havas PR, US; Ryan Foland, Managing Partner, InfluenceTree; Gini Dietrich, CEO Arment-Dietrich; Jeffrey Hayzlett, Chairman, C-Suite Holdings, LLC; Christina Martini, Partner at DLA Piper LLP (US); Scott Mordell, CEO, YPO; Jimmy LeBlanc/Perry Stagg, Louisiana Department of Corrections; Tim Sanders, former Yahoo! Chief Solutions Officer; Angela Maiers,

Founder, Choose2Matter; Miguel Dias, CEO and Co-Founder of CEOW-
ORLD; Peter Carrington, Saint Louis Barge; Simon Alexander Ong, Executive Coach and Mastermind Group Leader; Amazon's Alexa (yes, Randy and
I interviewed Alexa); Claude Silver, Chief Heart Officer, VaynerMedia; Peter
Fuller, President, Lived Fused and Vistage Chair; Trent Sanderson, Owner
and Creator of Team Prep USA; Benji Hyam, Co-Founder, Grow & Con-
vert; Cecelia Houser, Principal, Korn Ferry/Hay Group; Brian Solis, Principal Analyst, Altimeter Group; Tonia Ries, SVP Edelman, Executive Director,
Edelman Square; Robert H. Thompson, Author of *The Offsite* (Jossey-Bass,
2008); Brian Mac Mahon, Sensei, Expert DOJO; Sam Reese, CEO of Vistage
Worldwide; Jeff Hoffman, former CEO of Priceline and Partner and Founder
of Colorjar; Peter Shankman, Founder of HARO; Dan Hoffman, Founder
and CEO of Circles; Richard Franzi, Founder and CEO Critical Mass for
Business; Dave Peterson, Co-Founder and Partner at Play Bigger; and Chris-
tine Comaford, Leadership and Culture Coach. How's that for a dream team?

Thank you to Diane Stewart, Janine Drake, Chris Noonan, the Vistage
Chair community, and everyone else at Vistage Worldwide who played a
role in the CEO and key executive workshops I led throughout the United
States during 2017. I also want to recognize the many people who graciously
invited me to speak to their groups about the value of the people with whom
we surround ourselves, including my former Seton Hall University graduate students Jennifer DeBerardino and Heather Iden Faircloth. I hope you
learned half as much from the experience as I did.

I am grateful to my peer group in Lancaster, Pennsylvania, who inspire
me every day. We meet when we can over good wine and food, and it's always
a wonderful experience. Our members include Andrea Campbell, Marlin
Bert, Doug and Linda Weidman, and Mike and Molly Rowen. I also want to
give a nod to John Kenney, Pete Sciabarra, and Greg Wells and our priceless
Meeting of the Minds gatherings. I dedicated this book to my daughters,
Kristin and Taylor, but I'd be remiss if I left out the newest addition to our
family, Chris and Kristin Trawick's daughter (and my granddaughter), Nora.
I hope she grows up in a world where listening for understanding, learning
together, and helping others are central to her life experience.

Author

 **Leo Bottary** is an author, keynote speaker, and workshop facilitator on the topic of developing "peer advantage" for high-performing teams and peer groups. During a six-year tenure at Vistage Worldwide, Leo led the rebranding of the company and directed a thought leadership initiative on the power of peers, which resulted in a book he co-authored with Leon Shapiro titled: *The Power of Peers: How the Company You Keep Drives Leadership, Growth & Success* (Bibliomotion, 2016).

Leo also serves as an instructor for Rutgers and Northeastern Universities. Prior to that, he was an adjunct professor for Seton Hall University, where he led graduate-level online learning teams and on-campus residencies. In April 2015, he was named adjunct teacher of the year for its College of Communication and the Arts.

Earlier in his career, Leo served in senior leadership positions at Mullen and Hill & Knowlton, where he was also Director of Client Service for the US. In the mid-1990s, he founded a public relations agency that a leading industry trade publication hailed as a regional powerhouse, new media pioneer, and great place to work.

Leo earned a BA from Jacksonville University, an MA in Strategic Communication and Leadership from Seton Hall University, and has completed his doctoral coursework at Northeastern University.

Illustrator

As Managing Partner of InfluenceTree, **Ryan Foland** helps executives harness the power of vulnerability and authenticity to build a better, more relatable, more profitable brand. Recognized by *Inc.* Magazine as a Top Youth Marketer and named a Top Personal Branding Expert by *Entrepreneur* Magazine, Ryan helps thought leaders create and syndicate content that reveals their whole self to drive differentiation, growth, and loyalty. His 3-1-3® Method empowers employees to express their value in relation to the company and gives leaders a way to translate complex business systems into language that's relatable for customers. Ryan highlights the expertise of people within companies as the core talent behind the corporate brand, which drives reputation, trust and more clients to their businesses.

A student of keeping things simple and powerful, Ryan is also a stick figure artist. Starting as a personal challenge from Tony Robbins in 2015, Ryan creates daily stick figure drawings that both inspire and give insights into how to better communicate your personal brand. His unique drawings are very popular across social media and you can find them featured in children's books, business books, blogs, websites, news publications and more. Learn more about Ryan and the problems that he solves by visiting ryanfoland.com.

INTRODUCTION

How Will Doing *What Anyone Can Do* Help Me?

In 2017, Joe Henderson celebrated two fiftieth anniversaries, one as a full-time journalist and the other as a marathoner. Joe was a columnist and editor at *Runner's World* magazine for more than thirty years and has written more than two dozen books. He still teaches running classes at the University of Oregon and coaches a local marathon and half-marathon training team.

Back in the late 1990s, I became interested in running a marathon. I hoped to finish just one, only to run twelve more over the next five or six years. I was addicted to running, *Runner's World*, running books, and the life lessons they provided. It was during this time that I became acquainted with Joe Henderson's work. I have continued to follow him, even though I haven't run a marathon in more than a decade.

In his 1976 book *The Long Run Solution*,[1] Joe suggested that becoming truly accomplished at running (or at anything, for that matter) doesn't typically require us to perform superhuman feats. We don't have to leap tall buildings in a single bound. Success doesn't ask us to do what no one else can do. All too often, success and happiness find those who have the discipline to do the everyday things, the things anyone can do that most of us never will.

This concept struck a chord with me, and I never forgot it. I also never imagined it would find its way into the title of a book I would write one day. Although Joe Henderson and I have never met, I consider him and his wisdom to be part of who and what surrounds me every day.

What Are These Things Anyone Can Do?

To keep it in Joe Henderson terms, let's say you want to run a marathon. Until the 1980s, and well before IRONMAN competitions and ultra-marathons were part of the public consciousness, marathon running was considered extreme. It wasn't something most people would even attempt. Only a freak, or someone who lacked any other mode of transportation, would choose to run 26.2 miles. With the advent of Team in Training, which has raised more than $1 billion for the Leukemia and Lymphoma Society since 1988,[2] marathon training programs for the average person became more prevalent.

In 1994, Oprah Winfrey showed the world that if you surround yourself with the right people and follow a training program, you, too, could run a marathon. (She also lost seventy-two pounds)[3]. The real challenge, of course, is sticking to the strict regimen required to get you ready for race day. Those of you who have done it know that the race is the easy part, relative to what it takes to prepare for it—sixteen to twenty-four weeks (depending on the program) of the daily discipline to do what anyone can do on a given day.

The wonderful part is that when you do the things anyone can do every day for four to five months, you can accomplish something almost no one can do. That's the magic. The task is no different, whether you want to be an artist, a scholar, or a business leader. The question is: Are you willing to do the things anyone can do on a daily basis to achieve what you want in life? Because most people aren't willing, doing what anyone can do is the key to reaching any goal.

How Can We Do the Things Anyone Can Do More Often?

Wanting something is one thing. Being committed to doing what it takes to make it happen is quite another. Left to our own devices, we all too often don't do the work—or we don't do it over a sustained period of time. We might get off to a good start, but we eventually succumb to whatever rationale we can conjure that explains why we stopped.

Even the most disciplined among us can benefit from involving our friends, family members, and colleagues in helping us achieve our goals. While we all know that no successful person in the history of the world ever accomplished anything totally by him- or herself, we see self-help as by-yourself-help. As a result, we view our goals as solitary pursuits, and we don't do the things anyone can do nearly often enough. This is why we fall short.

One thing we can do is seek out people who can play a positive role in our success and enlist those people's support. When we invite others to be our partners in success, they tend to help us do all those things anyone can. This is why surrounding yourself with the right people is the gift that keeps on giving.

Surrounding Yourself with the Right People

Imagine for a moment you spent your whole life searching for the holy grail (whatever that may be for you), only to discover that the key to finding it and experiencing it for yourself was within your reach the entire time. For all those years, your family, friends, and colleagues were ready and willing to encourage you, share their wisdom, and help you realize everything you ever wanted for yourself in business and in life. All you had to do was ask.

Unfortunately, most of us don't reach out to others easily. In part, it's because we are conditioned to see life as an individual endeavor rather than a team sport. In school we are typically graded on our individual performance, and at work we are recognized and compensated the same way. Even when people ask us how our day is going, we often reply, "Great, how about you?," to which the other person responds in much the same way. We tend to keep what's actually happening in our lives pretty close to the vest. The problem is, if we want to realize our potential in business and in life, this approach simply doesn't cut it.

Here's one example: In 2016, a University of Scranton study reported that 92% of those who declared a new year's resolution failed to achieve it.[4] I suspect that most of those people set realistic goals they truly hoped to achieve. Among the reasons they failed is that they didn't enlist the help of others, of people who could have offered the encouragement, advice, and support that would have kept them on track and helped them do the simple things that could have made their new year's resolution a reality. As you'll see, it's these simple things—the things anyone can do—that really matter.

My Fascination with the People Who Surround Us

About six years after I sold Bottary & Partners (a small public relations firm I founded in 1995), I enrolled in graduate school. It's something I had wanted to do for a while, but I had never found a program that connected with my real interests. During a Google search one day, I discovered Seton Hall University's Master of Arts in Strategic Communication & Leadership (MASCL) program. I called the program director, Dr. Karl Soehnlein, to see if he thought I would be academically eligible (my undergraduate years at Jacksonville University were, let's just say, less than impressive). For whatever reason, Karl encouraged me to apply, and I was accepted into the program. I'm so happy he did, because the program changed my life.

Being part of a learning team alongside other mid- to senior-level executives was an eye-opening experience. In my previous educational endeavors the professors had lectured at us, but these acted more as facilitators. They realized that the students were a rich source of intellectual capital and that if they could create an environment in which students learned from one another and inspired (pushed) the others to be better, they could drive up the quality of the overall learning experience. They were right.

If someone had asked me at Orientation Residency if I believed I would graduate from the program with a 4.0, I would have dismissed the notion out of hand. In fact, that goal wasn't even on my radar. The only reason I earned a 4.0, and helped others do so, is because of the support of my learning team members, especially Dean Acosta. We did it together. Dean and I held each other accountable daily to the discipline required to succeed. Simple, maybe, but not necessarily easy. Left to our own devices, I can assure you neither of us would have achieved a perfect grade point average.

Today, one of the great joys in my life is working with students as an adjunct professor and mentor. In the fall of 2008, Seton Hall University was generous enough to hire me to teach in the program from which I had graduated. I taught for two of the online graduate programs, and, along with my amazing colleague Dr. Cecelia Houser, led on-campus residencies twice a year. I serve as a mentor for Seton Hall's Communication Honors Alumni Mentor Program (CHAMP), and I now work with graduate students at Rutgers University and Northeastern University, where I continue to marvel at the power of peers.

My Years at Vistage Worldwide

Shortly after I started teaching for Seton Hall, I accepted a position leading corporate communications for Vistage Worldwide, a private, for-profit company that assembles and facilitates peer groups for CEOs, business owners, and key executives, and their trusted advisors. As you can imagine, it was fairly easy to see similarities between Seton Hall learning teams and Vistage Groups. Both were composed of experienced people who shared a common goal and who realized that the more they gave to one another, the more they would receive in return.

Vistage Chairs across the country generously allowed me to visit their groups not simply as an observer but as a full participant. The value that the members received from one another's support was nothing less than remarkable. They learned together and helped one another envision their potential in entirely new ways. Just as I never would have believed I'd earn a 4.0 in my master's program, CEOs and small business owners took their businesses to places they never could have imagined. I watched in awe as they replaced their self-limiting beliefs with a vision of limitless possibilities.

After leading a refresh of the Vistage Worldwide brand in 2012 and creating the WSJ/Vistage Small Business CEO Survey, which remains in place today, I combined my academic work with my business experience to contribute to Vistage in a different way. During our engagement with the branding agency Neubrand, led by Bob Knapp, we realized just how admirably Vistage performs. This got me thinking that gaining a more thorough understanding of how and why peer groups work so well is the key to inspiring greater adoption among business leaders and educators.

Far fewer business leaders participate in formal peer groups than you might think, especially given their demonstrable effectiveness. In fact, if you tally the number of members of Vistage, Young Presidents' Organization (YPO), Entrepreneurs' Organization (EO), The Alternative Board (TAB), and any other organization you want to add to the list, and compare it to the number of business leaders in the world, you'll discover that formal peer group participation is miniscule. When you consider the transformational impact peer groups have on leaders and their organizations, the relatively low participation rate is hard to fathom. So my question was simple: If peer groups for business leaders are so effective, why are they so profoundly underutilized?

As one of the leading peer-to-peer leadership organizations, Vistage was in a unique position to explore how and why peer groups for business leaders work so well. I believed that if we could provide a framework and a vocabulary for the dynamics that drive the success of peer groups, business leaders might abandon the notion that they have to go it alone and instead choose to help one another drive new levels of excellence for themselves and their organizations.

This was the genesis of the idea behind my first book, *The Power of Peers*,[5] which I co-authored with Leon Shapiro, then CEO of Vistage. With the support of Vistage CMO Kathleen Delaney, CHRO Michael Molina, and the board of directors, we spent the better part of two years on a mission that was larger than promoting Vistage. Our book, along with prior works by Bill George, Keith Ferrazzi, Richard Franzi, Robin Chase, Henry Cloud, and others, serves as a small contribution to an important subject, one that I believe will attract much more attention in the coming years.

Why I Dubbed 2017 "The Year of the Peer"

Following the release of *The Power of Peers* in March 2016, and after speaking to business and academic groups across the country, I felt the need to drive a larger conversation and involve lots of other people. I wanted to encourage more people to contribute to this small but growing body of work on the value of the people who surround us. So I dubbed 2017 "The Year of the Peer."

Ryan Foland, a gifted speaker, personal branding guru, and cartoonist, challenged me to craft a narrative explaining my rationale for the Year of the Peer. He suggested that I outline the problem I was trying to solve and what

I hoped to accomplish. Here's part of what I shared on my blog post, "The Case for Adopting #YearofthePeer in 2017"[6] in late 2016:

> We're coming off the most divisive presidential election in modern U.S. history. As a society, we've come to debate more than dialogue, talk more than listen, and judge rather than learn. Trust in our institutions is low and the political climate for compromise has never been more toxic.
>
> Apparently, it's become more acceptable for our respective representatives (in Congress) to be intractable and come home empty-handed than to accomplish something that would actually benefit the American people.
>
> That said, blaming our political leaders is not a solution, nor is it entirely their fault. It's bigger than that. Collaboration and compromise breed casualties across all sectors—winners and losers, and leaders who "caved to the other side." As long as everything remains a zero-sum game, and those who collaborate to reach sensible compromise continue to be marginalized by the media (and the public), we'll all be the biggest loser.
>
> Neither collaboration nor compromise is a four-letter word. This is where CEOs have an opportunity to lead by example. Consider that, in 2013, a study conducted at Stanford Graduate School of Business concluded that nearly two-thirds of CEOs don't receive outside leadership advice. Seeking the help and assistance of others is a sign of strength, not weakness, no matter what position you hold in an organization.[7]
>
> Together, we have the power to send a message to every sector of our society that it's time for a change, because somehow, somewhere along the line, we stopped listening to what our elementary school teachers taught us all those years ago: We're simply not *working and playing well with others* nearly as well as we could. This is the problem we're trying to solve, and if we don't start now, it's only going to get worse to our detriment.

During the Year of the Peer, I engaged audiences during dozens of keynote speeches; I facilitated more than forty workshops with CEOs, entrepreneurs, and business leaders in the United States and Portugal; and, with the help of my *Year of the Peer* podcast producer Randy Cantrell, I conducted interviews with more than fifty thought leaders from around the world. My guests came from various walks of life, ranging from scholars and artists to entrepreneurs and CEOs. I surrounded myself with amazing individuals in 2017. You'll hear from these people, in their own words, as they share their experiences and insights about a simple idea: the people you surround yourself with matter.

The Purpose of This Book

This book isn't aimed at addressing the broad challenges of our society; rather, it focuses on the fact that, as individuals, we don't need to go it alone in this world. As you'll learn from our very successful *Year of the Peer* podcast guests (extracted directly from the podcast unless noted otherwise), there's simply no need to fly solo. None of these leaders did. So why should you?

Recently, I was asked, "Do you see your new book as a self-help book?" I believe the concepts in *What Anyone Can Do* will help just about anyone. I hope you will take the stories and ideas and help others. The condition of the world in which we live starts with each of us. The happier and more successful we are, the more likely it is that we can make a positive difference in others' lives. By focusing on how we can best contribute as individuals, we can align ourselves with the sentiment captured in airline safety instructions: "Place the oxygen mask on yourself before attempting to assist others." My dream is that, as a society, we will learn to collaborate more effectively to achieve what we want in life, work together to meet the challenges of the future, and realize the promise of a better world for generations to come. I believe we have that power.

Here's a snippet from one of my favorite scenes from the movie *Contact*, in which Ellie Arroway responds to her former mentor and nemesis, Dr. David Drumlin, after having a tough day testifying before Congress:

David Drumlin: I know you must think this is all very unfair. Maybe that's an understatement. What you don't know is I agree. I wish the world was a place where fair was the bottom line, where the kind of idealism you showed at the hearing was rewarded, not taken advantage of. Unfortunately, we don't live in that world.

Ellie Arroway: Funny, I've always believed that the world is what we make of it.[8]

I believe Ellie is right, so I thought it was worth writing this book and sharing the powerful stories and concepts I've learned since the release of *The Power of Peers* and during the Year of the Peer. These are concepts you can apply in your own life and use to improve the lives of others, because they're the things anyone can do.

How This Book Is Organized

As you'll see, *What Anyone Can Do* covers a range of topics and is divided into twelve chapters. In Chapter 1, I share stories and offer data from the Edelman Trust Barometer that show how our peers (categorized as "people like me") have grown in importance, and why, in the face of a decline in institutional trust, we shouldn't try to go it alone. Chapters 2 through 4 cover identifying what you want and surrounding yourself with the people who can make that possible. They also explore the tenuous relationship between expectations and goals, and how best to manage these dynamics.

Chapters 5 through 8 examine essential concepts that help us, as individuals, communicate more effectively, create safe spaces for deeper dialogue, and succeed in this world by paying it forward to others. Chapters 9 through 11 explore surrounding yourself with the right people from an organizational perspective, examining the value of being a good teammate, looking at what makes peer groups and teams really click, and showing how having a "people plan" can ensure individual and organizational success as we prepare for a transformational change in the workplace over the next decade. Chapter 12 offers conclusions, action items, and a few final words from the incomparable poetic voice Sekou Andrews.

Assembling the content for this book was a team effort. As it turns out, surrounding yourself with the right people matters a great deal. Enjoy!

References

1. Henderson, Joe. *Long Run Solution: What I Like Best about Running—and Do Most as a Runner*. Mountain View, CA: Anderson World, 1976.
2. "About Team In Training." About | Team In Training | Leukemia & Lymphoma Society | Leukemia & Lymphoma Society. Accessed November 26, 2017. http://www.teamintraining.org/about.
3. T-Rex Runner. "4 Fun Facts You Didn't Know About Oprah's Marathon." *Women's Running*. November 03, 2016. Accessed November 26, 2017. http://womensrunning.competitor.com/2016/11/inspiration/fun-facts-oprahs-marathon_67260.
4. McKelvey, Erin (Mack). "New Year's Resolutions Won't Make You More Successful." *Fortune*. Accessed November 25, 2017. http://fortune.com/2016/01/06/new-years-resolutions-successful/.
5. Shapiro, Leon, and Leo Bottary. *The Power of Peers: How the Company You Keep Drives Leadership, Growth, & Success*. Brookline, MA: Bibliomotion, 2016.
6. Bottary, Leo. "The Case For Adopting #yearofthepeer in 2017. "Leobottary.com (blog), December 18, 2016. https://leobottary.com/2016/12/18/the-case-for-adopting-yearofthepeer-in-2017/.
7. Larcker, David F., Stephen Miles, Brian Tayan, and Michelle E. Gutman. 2013. "Executive Coaching Survey." Stanford Graduate School of Business. August 1, 2013. Accessed November 3, 2015. https://www.gsb.stanford.edu/faculty-research/publications/2013-executive-coaching-survey.
8. "Quotes." *IMDb*. IMDb.com. Accessed October 10, 2017. www.imdb.com/title/tt0118884/quotes.

CHAPTER 1

No One Does It Alone, So Why Should You?

Since I'm going to ask you to reach out to the people in your life for help and to give of yourself to others, let me start. Here's my story, at least one of them:

Between 1992 and 1995, I led the public relations subsidiary at The William Cook Agency, which at the time was Florida's largest advertising agency. When I took over, the PR practice was hemorrhaging money. Within a year, I brought it to break even; two years later, it was among the firm's larger profit centers. I could do no wrong. Or so I thought. Displeased with some of the other goings-on at the agency, I left in November of 1995 to start my own shop. I didn't leave out of a burning desire to become an entrepreneur; rather, my departure was an act of immaturity and defiance.

I cleaned out my office on a Friday, and Bottary & Partners Public Relations was born the following Monday. I had no clients and a one-year non-compete clause in my contract with The William Cook Agency that prevented me from talking to anyone I had pitched in the past—and there was no question my former employer would hold me to it. Because I was highly confident that I could win business (and because I just didn't know any better), I opened my doors. Within a month, I acquired my first two clients. One of them came as a result of beating my old firm, which also pitched the business. A good start, I thought.

By early 1996, the agency began to gain real traction. It wasn't long before my client roster included the likes of McDonald's, Sprint PCS, CSX Transportation, Jiffy Lube, Jacksonville University, and the law offices of Spohrer-Wilner, the firm responsible for the first plaintiff's victory over a major tobacco company to survive appeal. We added new clients, realized solid organic growth, recruited excellent employees, and won local and national awards. To top it off, thanks to RAMWORKS CEO Greg Roberts and his talented web design team, our website was named Best PR Agency Website in America by Ragan Communications. So far so good, right?

It looked that way from the outside, anyway. In the past, leading a PR subsidiary inside a cash-rich advertising agency had allowed me to focus on my profit and loss without worrying much about cash flow. When I was with The William Cook Agency, we had well-established clients who paid on time, and I had a backup in case they didn't. Fast-forward to Bottary & Partners, where I had large clients who could take 90–120 days to pay, and the cash-flow situation was quite different. I continued investing in the business, however, hoping I could grow my way out of the problem.

Truth be told, I had real gifts when it came to winning new business and driving the quality of the work, but I had deficits and blind spots, too. I not only lacked the daily discipline (around the things anyone can do) that could have helped me ensure long-term success but, more importantly,

I didn't seek help from others to address my obvious weaknesses in both finance and operations. If I had joined a peer group of small business owners at the time, they probably would have looked at my situation and knocked some sense into me. Had I found such a group, Bottary & Partners might still be in business today.

Fortunately, on December 31, 1999, after having watched many of my peers across the country sell their boutique agencies to larger entities, I sold my firm to St. John & Partners Advertising & Public Relations. While my propensity for winning new business and leading teams helped me sell the agency, the business would have been worth much more had we been healthier financially and operationally. I don't harbor any regrets, as I have enjoyed career opportunities and challenges I would never have encountered otherwise. What's more, the enduring lessons I learned from that experience have helped me immeasurably in business and in life. As poetic voice Sekou Andrews once said, "You win some, you learn some." It's a great way to look at failure, so suffice it to say that in my life, I've learned a lot.

We Look to Each Other from the Start

Our need to connect with others is not just embedded into our social fabric, it's part of our biology and physiology. Infants require air, water, food, *and* human contact to thrive. Examples of how early this manifests socially among children are well documented.[1] To illustrate the point, let me share a story about my youngest daughter.

More than twenty years ago, when Taylor was about four and a half, the childcare center she attended held a Halloween party. As usual, I picked her up at the end of the day. When I arrived, I asked if Taylor was ready to come home, and the woman at the desk said the director wanted to see me. My mind began racing about the type of "incident" that would require such a talk. After a few anxious minutes, the director came out with a big smile and said, "You've got to hear what happened at our Halloween party today!"

At three o'clock, the staff had gathered twenty to twenty-five kids in a room adorned with decorations, where they listened to music and enjoyed a variety of Halloween treats. To add to the festivities, the center invited a witch to "entertain" the kids. Apparently, the witch looked a little too authentic for some of the preschoolers, so when she arrived one of the children got scared and began to cry, signaling to the others that something wasn't right. The crying spread like wildfire. The teachers frantically tried to reassure the class that everything was fine, but the children weren't buying it.

Taylor just watched as the scene unfolded. After about thirty seconds, she stood up, walked to the front of the room, put both arms above her head, and, as loudly as she could, exclaimed, "It's okay! She's not real! There's no need to be afraid! The kids looked at Taylor, looked at one another, and the hysteria subsided. Though the adults in the room tried to assuage the children's fears, the kids needed to hear from one of their own that everything was safe. Order was quickly restored, and the witch stayed at the party and entertained the kids as planned.

When I heard the story, I was obviously extremely proud. It's not as if I ever told Taylor that if the kids in her class get upset, she needs to step up and take charge. It was all her. Today, I look at that story through a different lens. The hysteria that overtook the classroom was not caused by the witch. It was the result of the first kid who responded negatively and then sent a signal to everyone else that something wasn't right. It stands to reason that a commotion caused by one of the kids could be most easily calmed by one of their peers offering assurances that they were safe.

Why Our Peers Matter More Than Ever

These two stories, of my failure and my daughter's success, illustrate the difference other people can make in our lives, if and when we allow it. I'm sure you can recall situations in your life when you've seen the power of peers at work, times when you could have asked for help and didn't, or occasions when you looked to others for comfort and guidance and found it.

In addition to my own anecdotal evidence, research suggests that, while our peers have always mattered, they matter today more than ever. One study, called the Edelman Trust Barometer, has been conducted by the global PR firm Edelman since 2001. This barometer measures trust in our institutions—in business, government, media, and nongovernmental organizations (NGOs) in twenty-eight countries. It's not a study about peers, per se, nor does it focus on the other important people who surround us, yet the nearly two decades of data make a compelling case for the fact that our peers matter more today than ever before. Let's look at some of the reasons.

The annual Edelman Trust Barometer results are distinguished by a headline drawn from the prevailing finding from a given year. In 2003, for example, the study noted that *earned media was more credible than advertising*. Rather than trust a company's claim about the excellence of its product or service, consumers looked to objective sources to validate such claims. In 2005, *trust shifted from authorities to peers*. So instead of relying on third-party media sources such as *Consumer Reports* or *Car & Driver* to describe the performance of a car, for example, consumers wanted to hear from "people like them" who had actually driven the automobile. By 2006, *a person like me emerges as a credible spokesperson*.[2]

During the past year, I've asked my workshop participants if they can recall *TIME* magazine's Person of the Year for 2006. Only once has someone known the answer. This may not seem unusual if you are trying to recall the name of a specific individual. What makes it unusual is that it wasn't a specific individual at all—it was *you*, or, more accurately, all of us. Somehow this fact has escaped our collective memory.

The release date was Christmas Day. The magazine's cover had a reflective material affixed to an image of a computer screen, so the reader could see his or her own reflection. *TIME*'s choice recognized the growing credibility of our peers, who were now empowered by technology to reach more people than ever before possible. If any of us had a good or bad consumer experience, we were capable of sharing that experience beyond immediate family, friends, and co-workers—we could share it with the world. We had become credible content creators with global reach. It was posited that we would change the world, which is why YOU were named Person of the Year.

For all these years, you probably believed that "you" wasn't specific to you; it was more of an "us" thing. You may have thought that, because you didn't earn this distinction entirely on your own, including it on your list of honors and awards would have been a stretch. That's understandable. So let me invite you to think of it this way instead: No other human who has *ever* been named *TIME*'s Person of the Year did it entirely on his or her own. All of those people had help—and lots of it. Here are a few excerpts from Lev Grossman's 2006 piece, "You—Yes, You—Are *TIME*'s Person of the Year," just to put your accomplishment in perspective[3]:

> *The "Great Man" theory of history is usually attributed to the Scottish philosopher Thomas Carlyle, who wrote that "the history of the world is but the biography of great men." He believed that it is the few, the powerful and the famous who shape our collective destiny as a species. That theory took a serious beating this year. To be sure, there are individuals we could blame for the many painful and disturbing things that happened in 2006…*
>
> *But look at 2006 through a different lens and you'll see another story, one that isn't about conflict or great men. It's a story about community and collaboration on a scale never seen before.*

I encourage you to read the entire article, but here was the kicker for me:

> *This is an opportunity to build a new kind of international understanding, not politician to politician, great man to great man, but citizen to citizen, person to person. It's a chance for people to look at a computer screen and really, genuinely wonder who's out there looking back at them. Go on. Tell us you're not just a little bit curious.*[3]

See what I'm talking about? If you don't have *TIME* magazine's Person of the Year 2006 on your resume or highlighted on your LinkedIn profile, you're missing the boat.

Decreasing Trust in Institutions

Fast-forward ten years from 2006, and Edelman began to see something remarkable: a growing gap in institutional trust between what it labels the informed public (those who are more affluent, have higher levels of formal education, and consume more news and policy media), who tend to trust institutions, and the mass population, who, according to the data, have come to believe the system isn't working for them and, as a result, tend to distrust institutions. This divide nearly doubled since 2015. The trust gap in the United States, Great Britain, and France, it turns out, was even higher than the gap globally.[4] Evidence of this lack of trust among the mass population was illustrated during recent elections in all three countries (Trump's victory and the movement created by Bernie Sanders; the Brexit vote; and the emergence of the final French presidential candidates, Emmanuel Macron and Marine Le Pen). There are also several other highlights of the 2017 Edelman results worth noting:

- Institutional trust decreased in all four institutions (government, business, media, and nongovernmental organizations) globally.
- 53% of the public believe the "system is failing them," while 32% are uncertain.
- Trust in the credibility of CEOs dropped in every country in the world.
- Trust in the senior leadership team is only slightly better than trust in the CEO.
- Fellow employees were found to be the most credible spokespersons.
- Peers today enjoy the same level of credibility as academic and technical experts.

Let's assemble these bullet points and paint a fuller picture. Institutional trust fell across the board—rated lowest in government and media—and a whopping 85% of respondents believe that "the system" is failing them or they are not sure what it's doing for them. NGOs and business are more trusted than government and media, but not by much. If people don't trust institutions, it's easy to see how the leaders of these institutions aren't getting much love either. Therefore, CEOs and their leadership teams are going to struggle when it comes to inspiring trust among their employees, customers, suppliers, investors, and others. When people don't trust institutions and their leaders, they look to one another, just as the kids in my daughter Taylor's classroom did, and just as the consumers I mentioned relied on other consumers when deciding which car to buy. People trust one another to help them make sense of the world. The more you understand this dynamic, the better you can harness its power.

Trust in the Opinions of Others

Gini Dietrich, CEO of PR firm Arment-Dietrich, alerted me to Nielsen's Global Trust in Advertising Survey (2015).[5] The study found that branded websites (e.g., Apple and BMW) are the second-most-trusted advertising format, behind recommendations from friends and family. Nielsen polled 30,000 online respondents in sixty countries to gauge consumer sentiment about nineteen paid, earned, and owned advertising mediums.

The survey elaborates on the trust of family and friends by stating that more than eight in ten global respondents (83%) say they completely or somewhat trust the recommendations of friends and family. But trust isn't confined only to those in our inner circle. In fact, two-thirds (66%) say they trust consumer opinions posted online—the third-most-trusted format. You should find this point particularly fascinating because such recommendations have become part of the way we operate each and every day.

When we refer to book reviews on Amazon, for example, we read the opinions of those who share our interest on a topic or a specific book. While we don't know any of the individuals from Adam, we accept the prevailing sentiment of these situational peers as a powerful data point.

On the consumer front, Altimeter Group principal and digital anthropologist Brian Solis shared this insight during our conversation on *Year of the Peer*: "To your point, the collective (experience) is more important than ever before. In fact, I've spent the last, oh, my goodness, two, two-and-a-half years now doing hands-on research with Google around what they call 'micro-moments.' We've been able to show in every single industry, including B2B, how shared experiences absolutely help someone make a decision about what steps they'd take moving forward before they ever engage a brand, or brand website, or content."

We are just scratching the surface of our reliance on one another. On one hand, lack of trust in institutions and their leaders drives us to look to one another when it comes to buying cars and books, or making sense of what's happening in the workplace.

But what about arenas outside work and consumer behavior? Are we inclined to address more complex subjects? Are we equipped to have open conversations about politics or religion, for example? Our capacity to engage one another on this level would appear to be an amazing opportunity. Taking advantage of this opportunity, however, will involve overcoming a few obstacles—the advice of our parents, the changing nature of news media, and a declining trust in experts. Let's take each of these obstacles one by one.

Exploring Obstacles to Conversational Engagement

How many of you recall your parents offering this advice? "Whatever you do, avoid talking to others about politics and religion." While this advice may have been well intended, socially speaking (and also served to avoid people challenging the nascent views kids were being taught at home), such directives did more harm than good. For starters, this prohibition assumes that these topics are fodder for hostile debate rather than productive dialogue. It assumes that when we engage in a conversation about our political views or our faith, an argument is sure to ensue, and that we can't simply ask questions to get to the core of why someone is liberal rather than conservative or how faith plays a role in one's life.

Imagine what we could discover and learn if we were equipped to have thoughtful conversations on the topics most important to our lives. Consider how less divided the world might be if we were taught to listen and learn rather than argue and judge. Unfortunately, because the notion that we should avoid controversial subjects was so embedded into our psyches as kids, we, as adults, often lack the ability to have respectful conversations without letting emotions run wild. As a result, we talk about comfortable topics and tend to surround ourselves with people like ourselves—hardly a recipe for learning and growth.

As I was growing up, my options for television news were NBC, CBS, ABC, and PBS. The professed goal of each station was to deliver an objective report of the day's events. If someone were to offer commentary, it typically appeared at the end of the program and was identified as such. Newspapers had news, sports, weather, comics, obituraries, and a clearly marked editorial page. Today, not only are the lines between news and opinion blurred, but viewers can select whichever channel best aligns with their worldview. If you watch MSNBC, it's likely you eschew Fox News, and vice versa. People today engage in affirmation rather than exploration.

Finally, Edelman's Tonia Ries says that it's not that peer credibility has risen as much as that expert credibility has fallen: "The 2017 Trust Barometer found for the first time that a person like yourself is now as credible as an expert on any topic, whether it's an academic expert or a technical expert. I actually went back and looked at the trend lines on that to see what the increase in peer credibility has been. What I found is that peer credibility has actually been flat, at about 60%. It is trust in experts that has declined, largely because of an increasing strain of anti-intellectualism that has fueled a loss of respect for experts and educators. As a result, academic and technical experts are regarded as less credible today than they were five years ago."

None of this helps us when it comes to being open to ideas from others that may conflict with our own, and I'm not immune to this inclination either, by the way. I catch myself leaning a bit too far left and not being as open minded as I should be. I listen with an ear for judgment rather than learning, and when that happens, I do my best to take note and alter my viewing habits and listening tendencies accordingly. When I do, I always learn something new.

We live in a time in human history when we have the greatest access to the broadest range of expertise and opinions the world has to offer. The more we listen for understanding—to one another and to experts—the better off we'll be. We just have to get a lot better at it.

Key Takeaways

During one of my *Year of the Peer* podcasts with CEO Gini Dietrich, she noted this quote from entrepreneur and motivational speaker Jim Rohn: "You're the average of the five people you spend the most time with." Dietrich said, "And I think that's really true, because if you surround yourself with people who push you to be your best self, you're going to be your best self. If you surround yourself with people who are satisfied with where you are in life, you're not going to do anything. If it's a peer group, if it's a Mastermind group, if it's an industry organization, surround yourself with really smart people who are going to push you to be at your best."

Use my story from Bottary & Partners as a cautionary tale and consider Taylor's Halloween anecdote every time you need to be reminded how much we depend on others to reassure us that everything will be okay. Combine your own experiencess with the data that unequivocally supports the idea that our peers matter a great deal, and remember that to truly leverage the power of the people around us, we should think about reaching out to others for more than book reviews and car recommendations. Maybe, just maybe, we can step out of our comfort zone and truly engage and learn from the people we choose to surround us.

We don't have to go it alone. And in this fast-paced, complex world, it makes no sense to even try. We live in a time when our ability to connect with people from anywhere on the planet has never been greater. It's something anyone can do. The trick is finding the kind of people who will both support us and challenge us to be our best at whatever we want to do. And what if you don't know what you want to do? On to Chapter 2.

References

1. Cloud, Henry. *The Power of the Other: The Startling Effect Other People Have on You, from the Boardroom to the Bedroom and Beyond—And What to Do About It.* New York, NY: Harper Business, an imprint of HarperCollins Publishers, 2016.
2. "Edelman TRUST BAROMETER." Edelman. Accessed November 25, 2017. https://www.edelman.com/trust2017/.
3. Grossman, Lev. "You—Yes, You—Are *TIME*'s Person of the Year." *Time*, Time Inc. December 25, 2006. content.time.com/time/magazine/article/0,9171,1570810,00.html.
4. "Edelman TRUST BAROMETER." Edelman. Accessed November 25, 2017. https://www.edelman.com/trust2017/.
5. *Global Trust in Advertising.* Report. Nielsen. September 2015. https://www.nielsen.com/content/dam/nielsenglobal/apac/docs/reports/2015/nielsen-global-trust-in-advertising-report-september-2015.pdf.

CHAPTER 2

The Power of Exploring, Discovering, and Expressing What You Want

KNOW WHAT YOU WANT, THEN GO GET IT. —RyanFoland.com

During a semester of study at Pepperdine I took a course taught by Dr. Vance Caesar, who shared with our class a video titled *Seeing Red Cars*,[1] based on the book by Laura Goodrich. Goodrich asserts that we get more of what we focus on. Notice one red car that just happens to catch your attention, and you'll start seeing them everywhere. Interestingly enough, Goodrich finds that when you ask most people what they want, they're often very clear about what they *don't* want but usually unable to express what they *do* want.

Goodrich, who today is internationally renowned for her work on organizational culture, was kind enough to appear as a guest on my *Year of the Peer* podcast. During our conversation, we talked about how individuals who want to surround themselves with the right people help themselves immensely when they are clear about what they want to accomplish.

Once you decide what you DO WANT, you need to surround yourself with people who share your goal and/or who have already accomplished it. These are the people who will encourage you, share experiences, provide advice, and help you stick to your daily schedule. Of course, until you pinpoint what you want, it's difficult to determine who all those helpful people should be.

Why Is Identifying What We Want So Hard?

In *The Power of Peers*, we addressed the challenge of identifying, expressing, and chasing after what you want by citing management consultant Robert Fritz. Fritz, known for his development of structural dynamics and his study of the way structural relationships impact behavior, asserted that most of us hold two contrary beliefs—powerlessness and unworthiness—that limit our ability to create what we really want. Fritz said he's only met a handful of individuals who are not limited by one or the other, and it's these beliefs that hold people back.

Brian Mac Mahon, founder and sensei at Expert DOJO, based in Santa Monica, echoed Fritz's sentiment: "Most of us are afraid because we're taught to be afraid. I've got a little boy who is eleven years old, and he still hasn't had the fearlessness beaten out of him, but he will. Over the next two or three years in school, he'll put up his hand to give an answer, and then a couple of teachers will tell him that that was a stupid thing to say, and then over time, he'll stop putting up his hand, and he'll become like everybody else."

Why Mattering Matters

Choose2Matter founder Angela Maiers's work on "mattering" serves as a brilliant antidote to the observations of Goodrich, Fritz, and Mac Mahon, showing that we can overcome our fears, address the challenge of identifying what we want, and share our gifts with others. According to Maiers, it's essential that we embrace our genius and allow neither fear nor humility to get the best of us because we all have special gifts to offer to the world, and it's our responsibility to identify them and share them.

Maiers explains it this way: "Five-year-olds believe they were born to make an impact. They wake up every day believing that until an adult in their world says, 'You're not good enough to make that impact.' We weren't born to embrace limitations. That is taught. Average is something that we choose. Maybe not explicitly, but subtly, we're taught to cover up, to hide and hold in our genius because it's not comfortable for the other people around us. We've got to stop that."

Maiers adds, "You are a genius, and the world needs your contribution. I watch as I say that line to five-year-olds all the way up to CEOs of Fortune 500 companies, and it is at about eight- to nine-years-old that I start seeing the first signs of people holding back. That is absolutely something we should urgently be concerned about, because the moment that our passionate people get quiet, the moment that the most brilliant ideas start being held back, the moment we don't start taking risks with one another, everyone loses. Not just the person loses—everyone does, and everything is impacted."

A Case of Mattering

It's hard to imagine a stronger example of someone who knew that he had special gifts to offer the world than internationally renowned inspirational speaker Rahfeal Gordon. Gordon, who spent part of his childhood homeless, moving from shelter to shelter and on occasion living out of a car, shared his perspective with me and listeners to the *Year of the Peer* podcast:

> Along the way, I knew I had something, I just didn't know exactly what it was. I knew I enjoyed meeting new people and bringing people together. I always felt like giving love was my core thing, that it was my brand to just give love and I would receive it back. I knew I had to do it in bigger venues and on different platforms.
>
> I used entrepreneurship as a way to (1) get out of poverty and (2) get into college. I was accepted to Montclair State University and started to just pretty much do the schoolwork. I wasn't a bright student, per se, but I was really good at networking. I was really good at learning. That was my thing. How can I be better? How can I assist others? That was the thing that kept me going along the way, and it got me to where I am right now.

Today, Rahfeal Gordon inspires people of all ages, bringing love, cheer, and hope to audiences on every corner of the globe. He particularly loves making a difference in the lives of young people. Here, he recounts a recent trip to Mexico: "I did a tour throughout Mexico. I touched about 1200 young people. I was just blown away that some of these young people waited two years to hear me speak. They've followed me on social media but they never had the opportunity to see me. Now they're teenagers. Some of them have jobs and they can buy tickets, and they can buy their own books. They come out and they just want to learn, and they say, 'I want to stay connected.'"

Jim Kouzes, co-author of *The Leadership Challenge*, described Rahfeal Gordon to a T with his depiction of learning leaders. Kouzes says,

> One of the things we know about leadership, exemplary leadership, is that you have to clarify your values and beliefs and have a vision of the future. The same thing is true for yourself as a learner. If you want to become the best at anything, you have to first see yourself in

that picture. You have to imagine that you can become better than you are, in the short term but also in the long term. So you have to look out three years, four years, five years, and say, "Compared to where I am today, I am going to be better at ..." and fill in the blank.

Gordon knew he wanted to share his gift for helping others. He pictured himself doing it, and he's one of the most dedicated lifelong learners I've ever met. Gordon had a calling, he knew he mattered, and he's come to realize that people of all ages look to him to inspire them to make a positive difference in the world.

Not Everybody Has an Obvious Calling

One could argue that Rahfeal Gordon had an instinctive belief that spreading love and hope was his calling in life. It's why he was put on this earth. For others, the road that led to their success was windy, rocky, and, at times, hardly much of a road at all. Here are three stories from our *Year of the Peer* podcast guests, describing in their own words their respective journeys.

Finding Your Luck

Paul Michelman, editor of *MIT Sloan Management Review*, talks about how he came to the job he loves:

> There are a million variations on the phrase *planned luck*, like "Those who are lucky put themselves in a position to be lucky." I think, to some degree, that's been true of me, but there's another piece to my story. I have two qualities that are alternatingly beneficial and detrimental. I am insatiably curious and I am incredibly impatient. The combination of those two things has—in ways I've only recently realized—been amazingly influential in the way my career has developed.

I see something new, and I drive toward it impatiently. That is not always to one's benefit, though.

More than twenty years ago, I spent a year working for the administration of MIT, where I'm happily back. My first stint was '94/'95, and I was part of a team that launched what we think was the first hybrid print/digital university magazine. Needless to say, it was not a successful endeavor. It was the coolest thing you've ever seen, but people were not, nor are they today, frankly, reading a print magazine and jumping on the Internet.

We did it because we could, and we were at MIT. Even the audience of people for an MIT-published magazine in '94/'95 were not ready for it. The magazine was one of more failures than I care to count, along a career path where I was trying to get out in front. Sometimes you calibrate well and sometimes you don't. That project was a combination of my impatience and my curiosity. Of course, I think it was also a really meaningful experience and I learned a lot from it. It's really important to be comfortable with failure—and I am—because you're learning things and you know how to learn things.

The way I found myself in the role I'm in today, which I am very lucky and grateful to have, is by being relentlessly curious about digital. By this point in my career, maybe I do have a fairly typical background for someone who becomes an editor-in-chief, but not entirely. I've moved from academic to commercial settings. I've moved from being an editor to being a product developer to being on the business side of publishing operations. I haven't done this with some end goal. I've done this because that's where my curiosity led me, because that's the next thing I wanted to do. I was an editor at *Harvard Business Review*, and it was 2005 and this new thing called podcasting was emerging. I said, "That looks like an interesting thing for us. I'm going to go try that." I launched a podcast called the HBR IdeaCast, which, long after I handed it to other people, has become one of the world's top business podcasts. Not that I take credit for that. It's just an example of my curiosity leading me to interesting opportunities.

Then came the app revolution. I just happened to be at the right place at the right time, at *Harvard Business Review*, to lead the development of the first set of apps and to create a product development group and methodology for *Harvard Business Review*. I kind of weaved back to being an editor because I became more interested in covering what was going on versus doing. There's been this weaving, and maybe the best way to capture it is this weaving between covering and doing that has no strategy and has led me to where I am today and hope to be for a while.

All in the Same Boat

Peter Carrington, owner of the Saint Louis Barge, took a nontraditional route to become proprietor of a floating hotel:

My background is in sales and marketing. I started in Ireland, in Irish textiles, did some training there, then moved to London. I worked in the London office selling textiles to high-end hotels, airlines, liner companies, companies like that. From there, I was headhunted by a company in New York, JP Stevens, and I carried on doing a similar type of work but in the European/Middle East sales regions. From there I was headhunted back to Ireland to work as Sales Marketing Director for a clothing company, a men's tailoring company. From there, sadly, local manufacturing became too expensive, and that came to an end. Production was moved off to Morocco.

I did what I knew. I became an agent for European clothing companies, some German, some Austrian, and one Danish. The Danish one also had a women's wear collection, and my wife and I got involved with them in retailing; they were keen to develop retailing in the UK. We ended up with some retail businesses. Then, along came the Internet, and that caused us problems. As a small independent retailer, it became very difficult, very quickly for us to compete effectively against bigger companies with bigger budgets, and indeed against start-up companies that did only online retail so didn't have the overhead we had.

Around this time, a very good friend of ours and his wife invited my wife, Wendy, and me to come cruising in the Canal du Midi, just as a holiday. Honestly, I did not want to go. I had a vision of caravans on water, cruising down these chock-a-block canals, very busy. Anyway, we went because our kids were at school with their kids, and that was fine.

After that, sadly, our friend's wife, Pamela, passed away due to cancer. We'd all reached a point in life where we wanted a change. Our friend was now single, and retail was getting very difficult for us. All our kids were going to universities. It was a natural time in our lives to do something different. We thought back to our cruise on the barge. Our friend wanted to buy one. I'd always been cooking, and Wendy has a design background. We thought, how difficult can it be to run a hotel barge? We are Irish, so we lack a little intelligence in certain areas.

We looked around and found this barge. Over the next six, seven, eight months, we put together a deal with the owners that allowed us to take over the business. The rest is history!

Creating Your Own Space

Poet Sekou Andrews thought he'd become a lawyer, but life had other plans:

It's an interesting journey. This life takes you on plenty of those. For me, it was a journey of pursuing the existing labels, as we all do initially. We pursue what exists because we don't know anything else. I do a lot of speaking on innovation and creative mindset and disruption and those types of things. A big element to those features is learning how to see the world through the machete-shaped eyes of a trailblazer, who stands in the middle of the woods and is the only person who sees the imminent path.

I was pursuing music, I was pursuing record deals, I was chasing Hollywood. Then, on the academic/business side, I was planning on being an entertainment lawyer. These are all existing labels. The entertainment lawyer plan was a backup to being an entertainer. If you work in enough law firms after college, you realize law is not really a backup; law is a commitment. I decided that I was going to shift to entertainment and pursue my passion.

So, I took a job as a substitute teacher, which is like the "actor/waiter job." The waiter is that job that allows the actor to go on auditions, right? The substitute teacher job was what gave me flexibility to do shows and travel if I needed to and so forth. When I took the job, I expected there to be world tours that I was going to need to be available for. (laughs) So I decided to become a substitute teacher and vowed that I would not become a full-time teacher because I had worked with kids before, so I knew I would love it, knew I'd be good at it. But I knew it wasn't ultimately what I was put here on the planet to do.

About eight months later, I broke the vow. I became a full-time teacher. I tricked myself into believing I was going to have all this free time as a teacher. I don't know what madness that was. Teachers have no free time. Shout-out to the real teachers out there who dedicate their lives to their students. I realized that I needed to make a choice. But during those four years of teaching fifth grade in South Central LA, something unique happened.

I started going to open mics to build a fan base for my music. I started performing my hip-hop lyrics spoken-word style, meaning I broke free of the cadence and the rhythm and basically delivered them through another vehicle and created a different experience for the lyrics that made them more accessible. It hit, and I hit, and I was a big hit on the scene. I had a rapid ascent on the spoken-word scene.

Then I accidentally fell in love with spoken-word poetry. That was not the plan. Not the plan, damn it!

But from there, I was like, "Well, now what do I do with this?" I joke in my speeches about how I was leaving a multibillion-dollar Hollywood and music industry for a multi-hundred-dollar poetry industry. But I couldn't shake it. I felt like I got more excited about... the entrepreneur in me, the pioneer in me... got more excited about pioneering new trails in spoken word than about being tossed into the sea of head-shots and demos out there pursuing the same crumbs.

After about four years of teaching and positioning myself and rising through the ranks in the spoken-word community and really learning from my peers, learning from the folks, that handful of full-time poets I knew out there, there was really nothing left to do but pinch my nose, close my eyes, hold my breath, and jump. So, I decided to do that and become a full-time poet. That was fifteen years ago this year, and I haven't looked back.

Being Open to Experience

I've told my daughters on many occasions that it can be easy to find *only* what you're looking for. The more open you can be to people and experiences, the more likely you'll discover the unexpected. That's what Paul Michelman, Peter Carrington, and Sekou Andrews were able to do so successfully. Cecelia Houser, Korn Ferry/Hay Group principal, echoed this sentiment about being open to others and to what's around us: "Too often, we operate head down, with blinders, because we tend to be so busy. And there is power in looking around and really beginning to see those people who, upon reflection, are really important to us, to see, truly see, the individuals with whom you spend the most time. And to also recognize individuals who might have had just a little bit of time with you yet have a profound impact."

Sometimes We Need Someone to Show Us What's Possible

Executive Coach and Mastermind Group Leader Simon Alexander Ong shared this wonderful story about Roger Bannister and self-limiting beliefs. In the early 1950s, doctors, scientists, and sports commentators were united in their belief that it was impossible to run a mile in under four minutes. After finishing the 1500-meter race in fourth place at the 1952 Olympics, Bannister almost retired from the sport, but hung on in pursuit of the unthinkable. In 1954 he broke the four-minute barrier by the tiniest of margins, completing the mile in three minutes, fifty-nine seconds.

Ong says:

> What's most interesting is not the fact that Bannister broke the four-minute mile. It's the fact that within forty-six days someone else broke it, too. Then, days after that, someone else broke it, because Bannister had shown what's possible. Suddenly, every other person after him said, "Actually, sub-four-minute miles are now possible!"
>
> It's the same feeling I got when I was in this group of people, or peers, if you will, from different industries and different businesses, from different walks of life. I was being shown what's possible. Because we work in whatever field we're in, we often get so caught up in that field that we can't see the forest for the trees. But when we expose ourselves to different perspectives, we open up so much more in our minds in terms of creative potential.

Key Takeaways

You can choose greatness by understanding that you and your special gifts matter to the world. Be curious. Don't be afraid to fail. Failing is learning, and we're all in the same boat. Be open to the idea that the most unlikely events can alter the way you see your life. Create your own space. There may not be a name or a category for what you want to do—at least not yet. You can create it. If you're good enough at what you do, people will appreciate you and your work. If you know what you want in life—or even if you need help discovering it—remain open to new experiences and identify the people whom you trust to share your hopes and dreams. You are capable and worthy, and, most importantly, you matter.

Leadership Coach Lolly Daskal offers these encouraging words::

When coaching individuals, there comes a time for someone who feels that they want to take themselves to the next level and they just can't. There comes a time when people feel challenged by where they are. There comes a time when people get frustrated by who they're being. So for every single person who has ever wanted to make a difference, who ever wanted to leave a legacy, who ever wanted to make an impact, I would like everybody to know—and I think you can get this from my book *The Leadership Gap*[2]—that greatness is not a destiny that's available only to a few. It's a destiny that comes to those who choose greatness.

Let's look next at how assembling your dream team can make your personal definition of greatness possible.

References

1. *Seeing Red Cars*. Performed by Laura Goodrich. February 18, 2015. https://www.youtube.com/watch?v=uXxMWvooPPA.
2. Daskal, Lolly. *The Leadership Gap: What Gets between You and Your Greatness*. New York: Portfolio/Penguin, 2017.

CHAPTER 3

Building Your Dream Team and Keeping Squares Out of Your Circle

RUN FARTHER

WITH FRIENDS. —RyanFoland.com

During the summer of 2016 the CEO of CEOWorld (now ScaleUp Academy), Miguel Dias, was kind enough to invite me to deliver a master class and participate in a peer group session at the ANJE Conference in Porto, Portugal. ANJE, which works with entrepreneurs and leaders of early-stage companies, was celebrating its thirtieth anniversary at the time. Before I left for my trip, Miguel asked me if I wanted to join him and my fellow speakers Rahfeal Gordon and Ryan Foland for a morning run in Porto. He suggested that it would be a wonderful way to tour the city and a fun means to get to know one another. I thought, "What a great idea!" I learned later that Rahfeal and Ryan accepted Miguel's invitation with equal enthusiasm.

We arrived at different times of day on a Tuesday. Ryan and I flew in from California, and Rahfeal took the overnight flight from New York. We met in the hotel lobby at eight o'clock on Wednesday morning, all recovering from jetlag but raring to go. Next thing you know, we were literally off and running. (Let me pause for a moment. You may be asking yourself the question we should have asked Miguel before we embarked on this self-propelled excursion. How far are we going? Turns out, none of us ever asked. Yet off we went.)

We just kept going, from the Crowne Plaza hotel through a lovely park that led us to the ocean (or the sea, as the locals refer to it), and then south along the coast. It was, as promised, a scenic tour of a beautiful section of Porto. At the turnaround point, we had already run about seven kilometers (or nearly 4.5 miles)—all downhill, mind you.

Before heading back, we stopped briefly to take a selfie. As we collected ourselves, we quickly realized two things: (1) We had to run back the same way we came; and, (2) because what goes down must come up (what I regard as the runner's law of gravity), the second half of our run would be uphill. Together, we ran back to the hotel, balancing a positive attitude with the common peer-to-peer axiom "misery loves company."

While you may regard this story as fairly unremarkable, consider this: Miguel invited us to run with him without knowing any of our running backgrounds or respective fitness levels. If he had asked, Miguel would have learned that it had been at least five years since any of us had run anywhere close to that distance.

Upon our return to the hotel, Rahfeal, Ryan, and I compared notes and agreed on three important points: (1) We all assumed (with a capital A) that it was unlikely that we would run any farther than five to eight kilometers, or three to five miles. (2) If we had been told in advance that we would be asked to run about twice that distance, none of us would have agreed to it.

Our self-limiting beliefs about how far we could run would have prevented us from even trying. Suffice it to say that it helped a great deal that we didn't know what we were getting ourselves into. (3) Had we not run together as a group, we would never have run fourteen kilometers on our own. It's a fitting metaphor for the power of the people who surround us, whether you're on a running tour or running a company.

Miguel, Rahfeal, Ryan, and I talk often about what we did together that morning. I credit our tour of Porto as one of the reasons we'll be one another's trusted advisors and good friends for many years to come. They are important members of my dream team.

What Anyone Can Do

During my talk with executive coach and mastermind group leader Simon Alexander Ong, he explained that surrounding himself with the right people is a full-time pursuit:

> For me, working to surround ourselves with the right people is part of what I call our daily rituals, habits, and choices. It's being conscious about who are we spending most of our time with every day. And what I say to people is that you can't achieve big goals and realize your potential if you don't have a group of people around you who will encourage and support you through that journey. You can have the vision, you can have the belief that things are going work, but if you're around people who are filled with negativity, then no matter how talented you are, no matter what potential you have, you can't help but be affected by that energy. I often say that every connection we have with humans, every business transaction, is about energy transference. When you're with someone who's very positive, you naturally get uplifted. If you're with someone who's negative, you tire quickly, you almost feel the energy sap out of your body.

Rahfeal Gordon agrees with Ong:

There's a study that talks about how if a person is motivating, they're inspirational. If you have a friend like that in your circle and you meet him for dinner or for lunch, his energy intensifies your joy. It makes you more excited about life because you're loving what this person is doing. You're proud of him and you're excited. When you move to the next circle, the next set of individuals you connect with, the inspiring person you had lunch with leaves something like a residue on you. So when you meet the next person, you have this palpable sense of joy. People ask, "What is that about you? Why are you so happy?" My thing was, "Well, I'm happy because my friend is happy. My friend is doing all these different things." That sense of joy is kind of like a signature of approval, showing that you have good people in your life. I think it's so important to have a healthy circle.

Jeffrey Hayzlett, CEO of C-Suite Radio, adds his thoughts about who should be in your circle:

I like people who challenge me and challenge what we do. I don't want to say, "Go find the guy who's the biggest pain in your ass and then invite him in," but to some extent, there's nothing wrong with that because that puts you on edge. It's just like a coach who pushes you when you're working out and sweating and doing tough things, and you think you're gonna die but you don't. That's when you have breakthroughs. I think the same thing holds true for your circle of peers. I like an atmosphere of open debate where we can argue, yell, and shout and it's okay.

The Aspen Effect and the Ripple Effect

Larry Robertson describes our human interdependency in the context of nature, as he explains the Aspen Effect and the Ripple Effect and what they mean for us:

The Aspen Effect draws its name from the fact that a stand of these beautiful white-barked trees with their quaking green—or in the fall, golden—leaves look like a lot of little tiny trees that are hanging together. Typically, there are about a hundred aspen trees standing together. They need one another to protect against the elements and to foster their well-being. Sometimes, a stand can number in the thousands. The thing is, there are not a thousand trees. There are not a hundred trees. It's actually all one organism. You don't see it on the surface, but underneath, their root systems are connected. They actually share nutrition, but also the anchorage in the earth to protect themselves from the elements.

It's that hidden connectedness that exists in an aspen stand that I use to describe not just what can happen as a leader builds a community and builds out into the ecosystem, but what actually *must* happen. This doesn't mean that you can't lead your organization successfully for a period of time without that interconnection and interdependence on others, but inevitably, that link is the thing that keeps you strong. That's the thing that allows you to weather cycles. That's the thing that allows you to anticipate, that interconnectedness underneath.

The Ripple Effect is very similar, but by contrast, it refers to the things you typically do see. As a leader, if I pay attention, it's pretty easy to see how my actions affect others. That may include others on my team, all the way out to others in my community and beyond. What's interesting to me about the Ripple Effect is that it's supposed to be apparent but often isn't. With the Aspen Effect, you look at the phenomenon and say, "Yeah. There are all sorts of things underneath the surface, all sorts of ways we're connected. I forgot about that or I hadn't thought about it."

The Ripple Effect is something that you see active in your world every day if you look. The number of people who stop looking or forget to come back and look to see if the ripples are happening in the same way, or what ripples are coming back at them from other organizations, is a lot higher than you would think.

The Inventory Check—Keeping Squares Out of Your Circle

Elite running coach Trent Sanderson asks his athletes to take stock of the people in their lives and shed the negative influencers: "We had a camp that went from four nights, nine nights, twenty nights, and forty-two nights, and it included around 160 student athletes from forty-two states. I picked a date and I told them, 'Okay, what I want you to do by this date is to disassociate yourself with someone who is potentially not benefiting you and not motivating you to become a better version of yourself.' What I try to teach them is, you become the norm of the group you hang around. I honestly believe that."

Rahfeal Gordon advocates what he calls the inventory check: "You should always inventory check who you're connected to and who you allow into your circle. You have to remember that you have twenty-four hours in a day and you want to make sure that the majority of your time is being invested well. Having a healthy circle will always keep you in shape."

After Rahfeal explained to me how circles inspire his life, I played a story back to him about what it was like for me when I met him for the first time:

Two things were very apparent from our conversation: one is that the joy you talk about is the real deal. When you get up on stage and you do what you do, I think to myself: "That's who that guy is all the time." That's what was really inspiring for me to see. The other thing you did, if you remember, was when we were walking around the streets of Portugal. You basically said to me, "Hey, share a quote with me. Share something that mattered to you or that you learned." In so many words, you were saying, "All right, teach me something." You told me "We're walking around here, I want to learn something. Tell me what you have." I think that is a really great practice. You asked others the same question. You challenged the people around you to bring some value, but in the most positive way, which was great. We encounter people all the time that we can learn so much from but we don't ask them. You asked.

Fortunately, I remain part of Rahfeal's circle today, and he is always asking!

Little Things You Can Try to Expand Your Circle

Altimeter Group principal Charlene Li says, "Peers are really hard to find, so when you find them, treasure those relationships and invest in them because they will serve you so well. It's worth every single minute, every single penny that you spend on them." So how do we find these peers? How do we extend our reach to create these circles and build our dream team? Our *Year of the Peer* guests offered a number of outstanding suggestions.

Making New Connections

JJ Ramberg, host of MSNBC's *Your Business*, takes time out to cultivate her circle:

> The following suggestion came from a guy named Ari Wallach, who I respect tremendously. He's done all this great stuff in his career. He said every week he goes for coffee with somebody new, and if he runs out, if the flow of new people has slowed down a little bit, he just goes on LinkedIn, finds a friend of a friend, and says, "Do you want to have coffee?" It's such a good idea. If you want to get people with different perspectives, it's easy enough. Go find them. It's not that hard, find them on LinkedIn, through friends, at a party. Just ask them for a coffee or a drink.

JJ also says that if you're going to an event, follow Eric Coffman's advice about arriving early:

> Eric Coffman is the most outgoing person I have ever met, and the most friendly. Everyone gravitates toward him. He said, and this was

so brilliant, for those of us who are a little shy (and by the way, almost everyone is at some point), if you go to an event after everyone's already there, which is your inclination if you feel a bit uncomfortable, everyone's already in their groups of three or two or five and it's really uncomfortable to worm your way into those conversations. If you are one of those first awkward people there in the beginning when no one else is there, you find your group because everybody is talking to each other because no one else is there. It's so counter-intuitive and so smart.

The Value of Curiosity

Co-author of *The Leadership Challenge*[1] Jim Kouzes, embraces his natural interests to help him forge new connections.

There's a wonderful book, called *A Curious Mind*,[2] by Brian Grazer, a Hollywood producer who has worked on many movies like *Apollo 13* and others. In that book, Grazer talks about the help he got by being curious. He made a habit of having a curious conversation about once a week, and I love that. He would pick people who knew more than he did, whether it was about movies or something he was interested in as a business executive, and he would make an appointment to sit down and have a conversation with them. That habit is one that he built up very early in his career, when he got his first job. He decided that he would, throughout his career, set up specific times to sit down with people and get curious, ask them questions, and essentially interview and have a dialog with them.

Pay Attention to the People Around You

Jeff Hoffman, former CEO of Priceline, and partner and co-founder of Colorjar, takes the opportunity to meet people everywhere he goes:

Amazing people are all around you and you're walking right past them in the store, passing them on the street, and standing in line with them at Starbucks, but you both stand there silently. Don't do that. Take the time to talk with people. One thing I've done my whole life is I engage everybody, everywhere. Strangers. If I'm standing in the Starbucks line, I turn and say, "What do you do?" Not everybody will engage, but I've met some amazing people, completely by accident, because I was engaging people everywhere. The more you do that, the more chances you have to find the people who will elevate and change your life.

Meeting and Helping Others

Founder of Help A Reporter Out (HARO) Peter Shankman leverages his outgoing personality to form new relationships:

I talk to everyone. It's part of my ADHD, and if you're on a plane next to me, unless you faked your death, I'm going to know everything about you by the time we land. And that tendency comes from my life and from what I've worked on. So, I'm very good at being able to focus on where I know people, how I know them, what I can take, and how I can help them. I'd always been connecting people, on principle. That's what I do. And I realized there was probably a better way to do it. There were so many people calling me, saying, "Hey, how can I …?" Help A Reporter Out, a service that helps reporters identify industry and academic experts who provide background and advice for their news stories, was founded out of that. And it became a no-brainer, as it were.

Be a Super Connector

There may be no one who understands, appreciates, and practices the art of being a super connector better than former Yahoo Chief Solutions Officer Tim Sanders:

Networking is something you do once you've developed trust. The difference, in my mind, between being a networker and a super connector is that the networker sees meeting people as a shortcut to success or a stepping-stone to success. So I think of the networker as a prospector in sheep's clothing. Networkers are out looking for opportunities and showing interest because that's how you generate a conversation, but ultimately, they go to networking events to meet new people to generate new opportunities, right? That's a networker. That's why so many people aren't into networking events.

A super connector is different. When you share your network of relationships, you're connecting other people who should meet. The super connector sees networking as an opportunity to give the ultimate gift to the world. The super connector takes pleasure in introducing the people who should meet, getting them fused, and then dropping out. Expecting nothing in return, having an absolute sense of humility, if you are a super connector you see that even though you introduced two others, that act didn't, of itself, create anything. The people had to act on that introduction for it to become something. You're not a prospector, and you're also not a broker. You're a connector.

Unnetworking

Super connecting helps us extend our reach, while "unnetworking" helps us build deeper relationships from the start. Unnetworking is an approach advocated by coaches Thais Sky and Bri Seeley. Sky shares: "When Bri and I met, we instantly became friends. I professed to her my dislike for networking and she has her own stories about trauma over networking. We decided to throw a dinner party and to put together some events to support women in finding a different way of connecting. It started with just one happy hour experience."

Seeley added, "We found, very quickly, that when women led with what they're passionate about, or are excited about, or what they're creating in the moment, a deeper and faster level of intimacy and connection developed between them than if they had just gone around the table and said, 'I'm a lawyer, accountant, blah blah blah, blah.'"

Sky goes on:

It's so easy for us to stereotype people into what they do. Once we know that you do something, and we don't vibe with that or we don't understand it, we don't really know where to go. Somebody says, "I'm a chemical engineer," and you fake interest because you want to be nice. "Yeah, that sounds great," but you really just missed an opportunity to connect with someone.

The crux of a successful business, as any successful businessperson will tell you, is your network. It's your connections. It's your ability to be in a relationship with other people. Business is all about relationships, right? We know this. Yet, many of us want to hide behind our computer. Many of us want to be on social media and pretend like we're creating a change in that capacity. That's not how it works.

We found that through unnetworking we remove that veil and avoid putting ourselves on a pedestal that consists of our business title—by getting people talking about their passions, we allow them to connect in a deeper way.

Key Takeaways

As I learned in Portugal, not realizing what you're getting yourself into can help you accomplish something you may never have attempted otherwise. Find people to join your circle and be part of your dream team. Join other people's circles as well. Don't forget to keep squares out of your circle. Negative people will only hold you back. Follow the advice of our podcast guests when it comes to staying curious and engaging others. You never know who you'll meet next. Become a super connector, and consider unnetworking as an approach for developing deeper and more meaningful relationships.

Sekou Andrews tells us, "You've all heard various versions of the phrase, 'If you're the smartest the person in the room, you're in the wrong room.' The one I always say is, 'If you want to be the best, surround yourself with the best.' I also say, 'Good people beget good people.' So, surround yourself with people you consider to be really great people because, more than likely, they will keep you on the path you want to be on."

It's the people with whom you surround yourself who will help you successfully navigate the competing forces of expectations and goals. The stronger your relationships, the better. Time to climb a mountain now.

References

1. Kouzes, James M., and Barry Z. Posner. *The Leadership Challenge*. 6th ed. Hoboken, NJ: John Wiley & Sons, 2017.
2. Grazer, Brian, and Charles Fishman. *A Curious Mind: The Secret to a Bigger Life*. New York: Simon & Schuster Paperbacks, 2016.

CHAPTER 4

The Yin and Yang of Expectations and Goals

More than fifteen years ago my teenage daughters asked me about climbing a peak in Crested Butte, Colorado—though it still seems like just yesterday. They imagined themselves standing on the top of a mountain with the kind of 360-degree view that you can't get just anywhere. Of course, standing on the peak is one thing, getting there is quite another. I talked to them about what it would take to prepare for the climb, and a few weeks later took them to Mount Baldy. At 12,805 feet, it was a challenging but reasonable climb for first-timers.

We left the house by 6:00 am to begin what would be a roughly three-hour ascent. The reason behind such an early departure? A good rule of thumb is that you want to be off the mountain by noon, in the event of an afternoon thunderstorm. The last place you want to be during such weather is on a big rock!)

As we began the climb, the girls were very enthusiastic. Now, if you've ever climbed a mountain, you know that in addition to the physical challenge, there's a psychological one. Because of the tendency to fix your eyes on the peak, it's easy to climb for twenty or thirty minutes and feel as if you're making no progress at all. Focusing on a goal that, despite pretty intense physical effort, continues to look unattainable can be very discouraging. So after about ninety minutes, I started hearing comments like, "the view looks pretty good from here" and "should we be concerned about those clouds coming in?" You could see the exhaustion on their faces. I suggested, "Let's give it another twenty minutes and see how you feel." (In fairness, the climb was not an easy one). Twenty minutes later, the summit looked no closer and the climb was getting even tougher. They were ready to turn back.

I then suggested that, rather than stare at the summit, they take note of where we were, climb for fifteen more minutes, and reassess. If they wanted to quit then, they could. They reluctantly agreed. After fifteen minutes, the summit didn't look any closer, but when I asked them to locate the bush we used to mark our start position, they couldn't believe how far away it was. They were astonished at their progress. So much so, that they not only felt a surge in their mental and physical energy, they also (best of all) stopped complaining. Once the girls reached the summit, they realized that there's nothing quite like the view from the top. Their feeling of personal accomplishment was even higher than the peak itself.

To this day, my daughters continue to draw upon this experience. Whenever they are faced with a tough challenge, they remember what they did that day. They approach whatever goal they are trying to achieve by celebrating their progress rather than being discouraged by the difficulty or the time it may take to reach the goal.

The Way We See Challenges Impacts Our Ability to Meet Them

Mental reframing, as we did during our mountain climb, can be very powerful in battling the yin and yang of expectations and goals. The wonderful thing about surrounding yourself with really great people is that they will teach you transformational techniques for meeting tough challenges in life and in business—and they can do this whether they are physically right there beside you or not. Here's another example of how a small change in mindset can deliver big results, whether you're running a race or embarking on a major strategic initiative at your company.

I was in my late thirties when I ran my first marathon. At the end of that race, I swore I'd never do it again, only to run twelve more over the next five years. Sometimes, on long run days or even during a few races, if I was not feeling 100% physically or was just mentally beaten down by the distance, I would stop and walk for a while, run until I couldn't run anymore, and walk again. I'd repeat the process until I reached the end of my training run or, in the case of a race, the finish line. This is how most people who are determined to finish make it when they're faced with hard times, when they're just having one of those days. While I may have finished using this method, the experience was not only debilitating during the run, it didn't help my confidence or do much to build my mental toughness for the next time.

A fellow runner told me that this can happen to anyone, but that I was thinking about it all wrong. He said that if you have to stop and walk, that's fine, but when you start running again, don't run until you can't go another step. When you do that, you're engaging in a mental exercise of repeated failure. Instead, when you feel good enough to start running again, look ahead of you and spot a tree or a stop sign. Set that as your goal. Run to it and declare victory. Start walking again, and when you're ready, identify another marker. Run to that and call it a win. He advised that declaring victory, rather than succumbing to repeated defeats, would help me finish more quickly and with a healthier attitude. It put me in control of the run instead of allowing the run to control me. The recurring victories would actually bolster my confidence for the future. Of course, he was right. It works brilliantly.

In fact, I offered this advice to my daughter Kristin during her first attempt at running a half marathon. I saw her with about two miles to go, and she was struggling. While I was loath to provide tips during a race, I explained the "declare victory versus admit defeat approach" to getting across the finish line. She tried it and was extremely grateful for the way this small change in mindset helped her complete the race that day.

Changing Our Mindset Works in Business, Too

Now think about this strategy from a business perspective. You set a lofty goal, have a solid plan to achieve that goal, and then set forth on your journey with all the energy in the world. As you run into difficulties along the way, your enthusiasm yields to your current circumstances and the reality of the long slog ahead. You start to believe that the situation is controlling you, instead of the other way around. When this happens, don't be afraid to walk for a bit, set a short-term goal, achieve that goal, declare victory, and set a new short-term goal. John Kotter, professor emeritus at Harvard Business School, has written extensively about the importance of generating and recognizing small wins.[1] The advice on running I received from my peer is simply a metaphor for why it's so effective regardless of the situation. Just keep putting one foot in front of the other and declare victory as often as possible.

During my conversation with JJ Ramberg, she shared this nugget of wisdom with me: "Someone a couple weeks ago told me, 'Don't let your dreams become your expectation.' They said that when things are going great, your dreams become your expectation. When things are hard, they stay dreams and it's something to work for. That really crystallized something that I felt I could understand through all the entrepreneurs that I've spoken to over the past ten years."

Rahfeal Gordon echoed a similar sentiment when it comes to expectations and goals: "I live by standards, not expectations. When I was writing *Skyscraper*,[2] I said, 'Okay, my standard is going to be quality. I want to make sure that every page has some type of strong insight that someone can learn from. I want to make sure I don't cut corners. I want it to be a really strong book.'"

Don Bennett's Vision of the Future

The relationship between expectations and goals was powerfully illustrated by Jim Kouzes, who shared the story of Don Bennett. The first amputee to climb Mt. Rainier (14,210 feet), Bennett accomplished this feat with one leg and two crutches. Kouzes says,

> When we first interviewed Don, I asked him, "How did you make that climb?" And he looked down at his one foot, one good leg, and he said, "Well, I imagined myself being on top of that mountain one thousand times in my mind every day, so I would have a clear vision of the future. But when I started to climb it, I looked at my one good leg and thought, anyone could hop from here to there, and so I did." And so Don took it one step at a time. We don't have to think about our goal as one giant leap ahead, we take it one hop at a time, make one small improvement at a time.

> As leaders, learning leaders, we need to get clear about how we want to see ourselves five, ten, fifteen, twenty years down the road. We need to know the kind of leader we want to become, that ideal leader—but then we have to take a look at what in the next hop we can do to improve ourselves. We have to ask: What can I do by tomorrow to be a better leader tomorrow than I am today?

How Can We Manage Expectations and Goals in Life?

If you find it unsatisfying to hear advice that suggests hanging with the right people, taking one step at a time, and keeping your eyes open for possibilities will get the job done, Peter Fuller, Live Fused CEO and Vistage Chair, has an idea for you. It starts with developing an outcome statement—a detailed account for what you want your life to look like at a given point in time—and creating a subsequent plan for making it happen. Fuller likes using a three-year time-frame:

> The best outcome statements are the most detailed. So, "The year is 20XX and I am driving this car. I have this type of relationship with my significant other. I have this type of relationship with my children. I am vacationing this many times on this kind of vacation worth $40,000 or $30,000." Put as much detail as you can into it— precise statements are the most powerful ones and are going to create the best results because your mind's going to start solving for those problems.
>
> While some of us have a calling and others (most of us, perhaps) have our lives revealed to us in some manner or form, I've been told by a guy who is a commander in the Delta Force, the elite of the elite, that writing his outcome statement was the hardest thing he's ever done. And these guys are drowned as part of their training. I don't know if he's being facetious; I hope so.
>
> Writing an outcome statement is hard to do because we don't actually ask ourselves what it is we want. A lot of business leaders don't ask themselves what it is they actually want out of life. Where do you want to be in three years? This encompasses your personal life and your professional life, not just your business. Any business leader can say, "Oh, well, I want higher profits and higher revenue, higher profits and lower turnover." We can all say that. That's easy. But that's not what this is about.

The outcome statement is the key. It's extremely powerful. It's based on a lot of psychology, but there are a couple of components in the outcome statement. One is the term. The term is three years, and three years max. Now, there's a reason for that. I won't get into a lot of the details, but the mind can wrap itself around the number three. You can go through basically the entire universe and the number three repeats in geometry and everything else. And so there's something important about the number three. We feel we can accomplish something in three years. Five years is a little bit outside our control. Twelve years and twenty years, we don't comprehend. And so it's three.

The second thing is the intent. And the statement says, "The year is …" Let's say three years from now, "The year is 20XX and I am …" So it's a declaration of your intent, but it says "I am" for a reason. It doesn't say I might be or I'm going to or I plan to. It says "I am." So the language programs the mind, especially when it's repeated, to actually start to believe that what you wrote down is what you are in that time period.

The third component is, again, based on psychology: the mind solves the problems it's given. If you give the mind a big problem, it will solve for that. If all you feed it are small problems, it will only solve for those. And what I've realized and what I've seen, not only in my own life after having this outcome statement but in the lives of others, is that rings true. So when you read this outcome statement every day, you're giving your mind a big problem to solve. And your mind will pick up on connections that will solve for that problem throughout the day. It also puts into perspective the daily grind or the stresses that we have throughout the day. It puts those into perspective because we know we're working toward that vision.

And then the fourth component is that we break that vision down into daily things, so you feel a great amount of stress reduction knowing that you're working toward that outcome and that outcome is already there.

Finally, the power of peers is undeniably the most important component. Because we can have that intent, we can build the plan, but at the end of the day if we're alone it's a lot more likely that we're going to just shuffle back into our old habits and old routine. Having the power of peers around us with accountability is that ingredient that puts the match to the fuel of our intent and helps us drive it. So I've rolled this idea out in my Vistage peer groups, and it's been remarkable. Everyone knows one another's outcome, and every month they check in. What were you supposed to do toward that outcome and what did you get done and what do you need help with?

Group members don't just understand one another's personal and professional outcome statements, they hold one another accountable for doing the things anyone can do on a weekly and daily basis. They help one another put one foot in front of the other, and they celebrate their small wins together.

Slowing Down and Taking a Breath

Simon Alexander Ong shared a wonderful story about one of his clients and the value of painting a clear picture or, as Don Bennett suggested, identifying a clear vision of the future:

We started by just exploring some of the things that she wanted to explore, things that made her happy, and I could see her face when she was writing down some of her ideas and bullet points on a piece of paper. You could see her face light up or her smile come out when she was writing all these different things down.

That spark is the part I like about these initial conversations, because in life, most of us know what we don't want. Whatever that is. I don't want to work with this boss anymore. I don't want to work with this team anymore. I don't want whatever it is. I don't want to live in this situation anymore.

When faced with such a simple question like, "What is it that you truly want?" many people get stuck, even though it's a fairly simple question. And we get stuck because we don't slow down, we don't take the time to reflect on important questions like that.

I gave my client the space to really slow down, and to take the time to explore all the things that were going on in her mind. I told her to just put them all onto paper without any limitation, without any second guessing. Because our mind can be quite dominant sometimes; it can question you, "Is this really want you want to do? Can you actually do it?" So, ignore that and just put whatever comes to mind on paper.

She decided after this conversation, which was about ninety minutes, to then say, "Simon, let's explore this." But she could only commit to once a month at the beginning. Again, this was fairly new for her, so she wanted to see what it was like first. And the great thing is, fast-forward a year and she's moved out of her job in the health care company and she's now realizing one of her true passions, which is to become a photographer. She's always enjoyed taking photographs at weddings or events, and now she's getting paid for that. In January, she started getting her first paying clients, and now she's getting quite a few lists of people asking her to shoot their events.

The funny thing about this story is that I've now become her client! She was my photographer, shooting my last two events for me. It's funny how this evolution works, but again what was very satisfying was that the journey she'd gone through. She'd not only achieved the outcomes, which we now see a year-plus on, but also she changed as a person. She has higher self-esteem, she has higher belief in her capabilities. Also, she's more confident in sharing her work with people, but in her own way. She's found a way that works for her. She can share the journey and the work she's creating not just with her friends and family but with the public at large.

Key Takeaways

Our relationship with expectations and goals can appear complicated, yet when you think about it, it's really simple. On one hand, we want to be at the top of the mountain, but we're not always prepared physically and mentally to do what it takes to get there. Over the years, Olympic gold medalist Usain Bolt has been challenged to race by various people who believe they have what it takes to compete with the best in the world. Bolt's response to these challenges: "Absolutely not. I think over the years people always aim for the top. I've learned something through the ranks that there's a ladder, but no one wants to climb the ladder. They just want to get to the top of the ladder. They always want to beat me. But no, no chance."[3]

Our success in life is not about being handed the opportunity to race, it's about earning the right to do so. Herein lies the opportunity. Any achievement worthwhile will not be easy but—assuming you're willing to do the things anyone can do (knowing most people won't)—you will have earned the right to compete for your goals. Surround yourself with people who will help you reframe your journey (with a bent toward your positive progress) and who will encourage you every step of the way. As Peter Fuller tells us, develop a detailed outcome statement, create a three-year plan to make your dreams a reality, and enlist the support of others to make it all possible. Want to learn more? It turns out that we learn better when we learn together. On to Chapter 5.

References

1. Kotter, John. "The 8-Step Process for Leading Change." Kotter International. Accessed November 26, 2017. https://www.kotterinternational. com/8-steps-process-for-leading-change/.
2. Gordon, Rahfeal. *Skyscraper: Going beyond Your Limits to Reach Greatness.* Rahfeal C. Gordon, 2015.
3. Tsuji, Alysha. *USA Today*, May 6, 2017. Accessed October 17, 2017. http:// ftw.usatoday.com/2017/05/usain-bolt-laughs-john-ross-40-yard-dash-challenge-zero-no-chance-nope-lol.

CHAPTER 5

We Learn Better When We Learn Together

LEARNING TOGETHER IS MUCH BETTER.

—RyanFoland.com

How many of you have ever been a member of a book club? Even if you only tried it once, you've experienced what it's like to have a half-dozen or so people read a book and come together to talk about it. The more you talk, the more you realize that different people will interpret different parts of the book in very different ways. The content is viewed through the lens of an individual's experiences. Certain events in the book may stand out prominently for some, and yet are barely noticed by others.

Many of the readers may recognize particular metaphors at work, and when they're pointed out, the story can be seen in an entirely different light or takes on a whole new layer of meaning. At the end of two hours, every person in the room will have learned something new about the book that she didn't know before the group gathered together to talk about it. When we examine a book through everyone's mental models, we often become exposed to ideas and perspectives we would never have considered on our own.

Learning Together in School

Stanford's Dr. Linda Darling-Hammond, arguably one of the top education experts in the world, sat down with me as my *Year of the Peer* podcast guest. Early on in our conversation, I suggested to her that when I went to secondary school, we would have referred to collaborative learning as "cheating." I grew up shading my paper from my classmates. Learning was an exercise in what I could remember or understand without the help of others. Fortunately, this is changing.

Dr. Darling-Hammond offers this assessment:

There's a mountain of research on collaborative learning and cooperative learning. Done well, it is more effective in enabling students to both get the assistance they need as they're learning and to solve problems at a higher level of sophistication. That does require sophisticated teaching because you have to know how to organize group-worthy tasks and set rules for students and enable them to learn to do that work.

We've all had bad experiences with group work, when somebody just throws a bunch of people at a problem and one person does all the work and the other people sit and watch. That's because, quite often, the pedagogical practices that are needed are not in place. When they are, peers learn beautifully together, and you see that with kids when they're playing and when they're doing things together outside of schools.

The same is then true, also, for teachers who, as it turns out, benefit enormously from collaboration. We have evidence both internationally and from studies in the United States that teachers are more effective when they are able to meet and plan and talk regularly and give feedback to one another, that they stay in the profession longer under those circumstances, that they feel more efficacious, that they're more likely to engage in more challenging kinds of practices that are aimed at higher-order thinking skills and problem solving for students. Collaboration is really the name of the game in terms of moving education systems forward. Teaching is a team sport, not just an individual act.

Learning Together in Business

With regard to learning and collaboration for business leaders, Leon Shapiro and I shared two important findings in *The Power of Peers*. First, we learned that CEOs who participate in peer groups bring the skills they learn from working with other CEOs to encourage and teach their leadership teams and employees to work together more effectively. It's not unlike what Dr. Darling-Hammond said about teachers. The more collaborative CEOs are with one another, the more likely they will create collaborative learning environments in the workplace (Figure 5.1).

Figure 5.1 *The learning–achieving cycle.*

Second, we created a reinforcing loop to illustrate why learning together is so effective. We *learn* best when we *share* concepts and ideas with one another. We help one another generate a deeper understanding and embed the learning. Better yet, we give one another the courage to act—to actually *apply* what we learn. It's one thing to read about a concept in a book or hear it voiced at a conference; it's quite another to implement it and make it part of the way we work going forward. Once we try the concept and work to perfect the new initiative, we can begin to *achieve* the positive results we imagined. The group celebrates member wins together, which only inspires everyone to learn more and repeat the cycle. (This is why CEOs who participate in this process tend to bring this dynamic inside their organizations, both purposely and subconsciously).

The Best Leaders Are Also the Best Learners

Jim Kouzes describes what he and co-author Barry Posner learned in writing *Learning Leadership*;[1] essentially, they discovered that the best leaders tend to be those who are most committed to lifelong learning. This practice of continuous learning tends to help them be better listeners and stay open to views that may conflict with their own. Kouzes says,

> One of the things we found in our research with Lillas Brown at the University of Saskatchewan, was that the best leaders are the best learners. It doesn't matter what style you use to learn, what does matter is how frequently you use whatever style you have. We found that those leaders who engage more frequently in learning activities scored higher on our Leadership Practice's Inventory, our assessment measure of The Five Practices of Exemplary Leadership®. We've known that for a long time, but we decided after more than thirty years of training executives that we needed to spend a little bit more time codifying what we had learned about how you learn, not just your learning style, but the environment and the climate you need to set.

We wrote a book, *Learning Leadership*, that explores what we call the Five Fundamentals of Learning Leadership, the five fundamentals of becoming an exemplary leader. The first of those five fundamentals is that you need to believe you can. If you don't believe that you can do something, you can't, because you are not going to invest the time and energy in it. You have to believe that you can become a better leader, and this first fundamental responds to the most important question we wanted to address. The single most frequently asked question we get when we talk about leadership or we train executives is this: Are leaders born or made? Because we have been asked it so often we have a standard answer. And that answer is, we've never met a leader who was not born.

All leaders are born, all engineers are born, all architects are born, all artists are born, all musicians are born, all computer scientists are born, and financial analysts are born. We're all born; it's what we do with what we have before we die that's important. So, the question really ought to be, how do I become the best leader I can be? And that was the question we wanted to answer. Instead of focusing on the practices of leadership, we ask: How do I learn to become the best?

The next fundamentals flow naturally from the first: the second is that you have to aspire to excel; the third is that you need to challenge yourself; fourth, you need to engage support; and finally, the fifth, you need to practice deliberately. Those are the five fundamentals that make up the basic chapters of *Learning Leadership*.

Communities of Practice

The need to engage support, as outlined by Kouzes and Posner, is fundamental to the learning process and aligns with the early work of learning theorists Etienne Wenger-Trayner and Jean Lave. Etienne Wenger-Trayner explains where communities of practice came from:

It started as an observational concept. It was not a technique in the beginning. It was just something we observed by doing studies of learning in natural settings. We noticed that people formed these informal communities around things that they needed to learn how to do together. We started with studies of apprenticeship—we had a master and then apprentices around the master. People were learning from each other, and we came up with the name Community of Practice. It's only later that we said, "Oh, that's an interesting way of learning. Could we use this as an alternative to classroom learning, since it's the way that people have learned together forever, since the beginning of the species pretty much."

During my conversation with Etienne and Beverly Wenger-Trayner, I asked whether it was fair to say that he and Jean Lave intended to focus on the relationship between the master and the student or the master and the apprentice, only to discover how much these students and apprentices learn from one another. Etienne replied, "That's right. But it's also fair to say that was where we got the idea, but then we found a lot of places where there's no one master. In many scenarios, there's more a general partnership among people."

Etienne Wenger-Trayner went on to say that good communities of practice don't engage in knowledge sharing so much as problem solving. Beverly explained it this way: "They share their challenges rather than their knowledge. They share challenges and work out ways that they can address those challenges better together than they can on their own."

Learning Across Landscapes

Today's largest companies can consist of complex matrices and overlapping systems, which has meant that the original concept of communities of practice has evolved. Beverly Wenger-Trayner speaks about this ongoing evolution:

Because we are consultants, more and more of our work over the last several years has come from people or organizations trying to make progress or address an issue, but where the people who need to come together in order to address that issue are not necessarily obvious learning partners.

It's easy if you're a group of engineers or a group that has a very obvious community of practice. We find, more and more, that organizations need people who don't always see themselves as learning partners to come together to address a challenge. A single community of practice is not big enough to bring together people across what we call the "landscape." In a landscape, you have multiple communities of practice.

If you've got multiple communities of practice, you've also got boundaries around the edge of community of practice and between those communities of practice. Very often, those are deep boundaries, very disciplinary, culturally. There may be boundaries between them, so when you bring people together, even though they are all trying to solve a common issue, they may have historic boundaries between them that need to be resolved. You need to turn those boundaries into learning assets, because building bridges and having conversations across boundaries are ways of moving the conversation forward.

Etienne illustrates the point this way: "You want to have very good salespeople, but the fact that the salespeople are very good and the engineers are very good is sometimes not enough. Sometimes there has to be conversation between them. You need to focus on where the boundaries are, because people don't talk across those boundaries. When we work with clients, we recommend that they look at the whole thing."

Looking at the whole thing means looking beyond one's immediate area, department, or practice area and considering how decisions may play out over a period of time beyond the immediate. Doing so involves connecting, communicating, and listening to all the stakeholders who are part of the whole.

The Power of Peer-to-Peer Relationships

Lewis Schiff and Jeffrey Hayzlett offer their perspective on the power of deeply embedded peer-to-peer learning relationships. Schiff says,

> In a peer relationship there's equivalency; you're trying to help each other do the same things. I think there are questions you ask peers that you might not ask mentors. I think with peers in a business context, you should say, "What are your goals? How much money do you make? How much money do you want to make? If you make 100 and you want to make 150, how many new clients or opportunities do you need to get there?" If I'm going to be in a peer-to-peer relationship with you I should be aware of what's important to you and be thinking about how to help you accomplish that, and you should be doing that for me. In a mentor/mentee relationship you wouldn't really ask how much money the other person makes or how much they want to make. I think that's the distinction between those two types of relationships.

Hayzlett adds his thoughts as they pertain to peer-to-peer relationships in a social context, and notes that these relationships have always mattered:

> It matters who you hang around with, who you associate with, who you socialize with, because we learn through a process of socialization, which means we learn through our social interactions with other people and the people who are around. And that's how we become who we are. We do this with Facebook today, we do this with our friends, we do this with influencers, and that's truly the strength, but it starts way, way back. When I was young, I was hanging around a crowd I maybe shouldn't have been hanging around, and my mom says, "Don't you be hanging around them," and my dad reinforced that.

According to Hayzlett, he remains attentive to this day to the people he surrounds himself with.

On Learning How to Learn Together

We can learn a great deal by looking at schools around the world and thinking about countries that do collaborative learning really well. Dr. Darling-Hammond comments on how the best in the world enable collaborative learning, and examines how we can learn from these countries' effective practices:

> One thing that's often true in education is that if you want something to occur for children, you should make sure that it's occurring for teachers as well, because teachers can take what they have experienced and translate it for kids. It's very rare that you can get one without the other. Let me talk about collaboration among teachers first, and then I'll talk about students.
>
> One of the things that they do in places like Singapore, for example, is they have, out of the forty-hour work week, somewhere between fifteen and twenty hours for teachers to collaborate with one another. They're teaching kids about nineteen hours a week. Then they are working with each other on planning lessons, on lessons study where they develop something together. One teacher might implement the lesson in the classroom while the others watch how the kids are doing and collect data; then, they all come back and talk about how to fine tune the lesson. Somebody else tries, and that teacher is observed. They may do action research together where they take up a problem of teaching and try a new strategy and see what happens and write it up and share it with each other. They may be in and out of each other's classrooms observing and giving feedback. That's all structured into the workday for teachers.
>
> In the United States, our teachers are still on the old factory model from the early 1900s. Our teachers teach more hours per year than

teachers anywhere else in the world. They have more instructional hours per week with fewer breaks and less opportunity to work together. They also have less planning time than in most other countries, and the planning time is typically individual, so you might get three, four, five hours a week as a US teacher to plan your lessons and run your dittos or get your videos ready. Rarely are you scheduled with other teachers jointly to decide how to design the curriculum, how to design assessments.

The collaborative work in places likes Singapore or Shanghai or Finland means that the lessons the teachers do offer are very, very thoughtfully designed. There's been a lot of problem solving around the best way to represent the concept, the best assignment to give to kids, the kind of supports kids will need to succeed. Then, once the teaching has occurred, teachers can come back together and continue to improve it.

This type of cooperation, then, translates into work the kids are doing. In many of these countries, kids are also very explicitly collaborating. In Singapore, to continue with that example for a moment, as part of the students' formal assessment program they do a collaborative project, where kids take up a problem and figure out how to approach it together. That project is in lieu of a multiple-choice test. That's actually one of the formal assessments that they turn in and teachers are trained to score them on. They value collaboration so much they bring it right into the assessment system.

In our conversation, we also talk about how we learn by doing, and Dr. Darling-Hammond reinforces the fact that this is hardly a new idea:

In the early 1900s, educational reformer John Dewey began contending that experience and education go together, that people learn by doing and by thinking. It's the doing and the reflecting together that lead to learning. That is how human beings have always learned, by inquiring and then reflecting on what they've found, and then inventing and building on those inventions. When we, in schools, separate experience from education and say, "Sit at a desk and listen to somebody else tell you things," we're really reducing the amount of serious learning that will transfer to settings outside of school. It's a long-time problem and I think we have some schools making real headway on this, but we have to break the idea that education requires sitting at a desk and just taking in what somebody else says rather than trying, doing, inquiring, investigating, applying, learning.

Combining Doing with Collaborative Learning Online

Miguel Dias shared his recent plans on the evolution of ScaleUp Academy, which brings entrepreneurs together online to learn from one another about how to scale their businesses. Dias not only advocates learning by doing, he also believes it is essential that we learn how to do so together. He sees this method of collaborative learning as faster and more effective:

We have been discussing the model, which is growing from an online meetup or peer group to a real academy. And it is an academy based in peer learning, so it's not about showing up and teaching a course, it's about talking through individual issues. So a student has identified some issues he wants to work on, and that's why he's meeting with that teacher, with that professional. Because he knows that teacher or professional has been living these issues and has pragmatic experience dealing with them.

Students show up and say, "Look, I have an issue in my marketing department. So I'm putting some of my resources on traffic generation and I'm testing some growth hacking techniques. I'm working with a supplier. But I don't know if this fits into my business model and if I'm taking the right choices. Also, I'm setting up now with special units, which is the customer success unit inside my company, and I've never done this before. The CEO is pressing me a lot on whether the other worldwide, world-class companies are doing the same. I've been reading a lot, I've been talking with some colleagues, but I don't know where to start."

This is the kind of really pragmatic value you get. This kind of learning is not about sitting down and listening to a course or to someone talking about the topic of customer success. It's really working on your own issues and leaving the session with pragmatic resources and tools and experiences that let you execute with quality, which I think is the most important thing. When you need to make decisions in a leadership position, you have to be really clear about what you want to do and how to coordinate your team.

That's why the format of peer learning is so effective. You select the sessions that are relevant to you in that specific month, and you join any of the guests to discuss your own issues with your peers in a very small group, wherever you are. There's no need to go to a specific place to attend the session. That's where we are moving.

Dan Hoffman, CEO of Circles, has created a dedicated online platform designed to serve as a conversation tool rather than a presentation tool such as WebEx, Zoom or Go-To-Meeting. His platform has been created specifically to maximize the power of peer-to-peer learning online. He told me, "Leo, you've seen the magic when you get a circle of peers helping and giving help. Part of my mission has been to take that feeling, that fire that exists for about 100,000 CEOs across Vistage, EO, YPO, and some of the other groups, and ask the question, why doesn't everyone in the world have this? Why can't this circle idea be a structure that really helps people in all walks of life learn together and move forward in their lives?"

Key Takeaways

One of the strongest expressions of intent that I've ever heard about collaborative learning involved the concept of learning citizenship. Beverly Wenger-Trayner says, "We are developing a concept of 'learning citizens,' individuals who are using who they are as a vehicle for enabling learning around them. Not just their own learning is important—they also enable learning around them. Each of us is potentially a learning citizen. Related to learning citizenship is a learning ethic, which focuses on contributing to our own learning, that of the people around us, and of the world."

Starting today, think of yourself as a learning citizen, and share the power of that idea with others. Whether we're in a book club, a classroom, a peer group, or the workplace, we learn better when we learn together. As teachers and business leaders, the more collaborative we are with one another, the more likely it is that we will create healthy learning and collaborative environments for students and employees alike. It starts with asking questions and listening for understanding.

Reference

1. Kouzes, James M., and Barry Z. Posner. *Learning Leadership: The Five Fundamentals of Becoming an Exemplary Leader.* Hoboken, NJ: Wiley, 2016.

CHAPTER 6

Asking Questions and Listening for Understanding

Expert DOJO's sensei, Brian Mac Mahon, invited personal branding guru Ryan Foland and me to speak for a full morning session at the Digital Hollywood Conference in Los Angeles in 2016. What an amazing event! Mac Mahon delivered the kind of insight that can be provided only by someone who has lived in thirty countries and has consulted and started companies the world over. Foland, a gifted presenter in his own right, delivered a master class in communication for entrepreneurs. I reinforced the value of coming together for conferences and the need for extending that experience beyond the event through participation in peer advisory/mastermind groups.

During the final forty-five minutes of the session, we set up a spontaneous mastermind group composed initially of about ten volunteers; soon after we got underway, everyone joined in the experience. As I reflect on the two-and-a-half hours we spent with this impressive group of entrepreneurs, it's apparent that the most powerful moments of the entire session were found not in the answers given but in the questions raised. Answers tend to guide us to a conclusion, while questions promote additional learning and further discovery. The audience asked Mac Mahon some very pointed questions, questions that often got to the heart of what was burning inside everyone in the room.

Foland offered a version of the $64,000 question to the audience when he asked them to identify the problems their companies are trying to solve. He didn't ask, "What do they do?" or "How do they do it?" Foland asked the bigger question because, unless you know precisely what problem you're trying to solve, you're going to have a difficult time communicating the relevance of what you do—and thus you'll have a hard time surviving as a company.

After discussing the value of mastermind groups and why they work so well, we invited people to come up on stage and give the concept a try. We welcomed them to participate in a real-time experience in which one of the members asked the group for assistance in addressing her most pressing challenge. This is where the rubber meets the road. By taking a few moments to assist the member in crafting her question as accurately as we could, we prevented the group (this works most of the time) from giving the member great ideas that turn out to have no real utility, and which aren't ultimately much help at all. After helping the member frame the question, it was time for the group members to start asking questions of their own in an effort to gain a greater understanding of the situation. Here, we established just three rules for asking questions of the member seeking assistance:

1. Ask open-ended questions (ones that cannot be answered yes or no).
2. Do not ask "why" questions (in trying to create a safe environment for sharing, "why" questions can tend to put a group member needlessly on the defensive).
3. Do not frame a question as a "question-mendation" (meaning, ask questions that improve your understanding what's going on, not veiled recommendations such as, "Have you considered trying x, y, or z?").

Everyone jumped right in and followed my three rules to the letter. Best of all, the richness of the exchange, along with the ideas that came from participants after the initial question session, demonstrated to everyone that even in forty-five minutes a group of people—many of whom had met only that morning—could deliver and receive real value.

The Key Is Listening

I can't tell you how much I enjoyed listening to the insights from this impromptu mastermind group and to the roughly fifty guests who appeared on my podcast last year. I knew that the more I listened to learn, rather than judge, the better I would be at asking questions. I also knew that both the audience and I would gain more from the experience if I approached the topics with true curiosity and listened with care.

Here are a few of the highlights about listening shared by my *Year of the Peer* guests in their own words. Take in the following highlights by reading ("listening with your eyes"), and imagine hearing the sounds of their voices.

Listening for the Truth

JJ Ramberg underscores the importance of hearing what your customers are saying to you:

It's very easy for us all to just sort of shut our ears. You talked about this tendency politically or socially right now, but it's also true in business. If someone says to you, "Hey, I think you should be doing this differently," or, "This is how I reacted to that piece of marketing that you put out," it's really easy to say, "Oh, you just don't get it." But if someone's saying that he doesn't relate to the way you're describing your company, you better listen and see if there's actually some truth to it that goes beyond this one person.

The Importance of the Why Behind the Words

Rahfeal Gordon notes the relationship between our role in a person's life and what the person truly needs:

> I think it's important to listen. I think it's very important that we, as individuals, take time to understand why a person does what he does. You ask questions that allow you to get an understanding of the person—even if you don't agree with some of the things— so you understand what the person's belief systems are, what his standards are, and how that plays a part in expectations. Often, I think we can have these high expectations, or have these visions for people, because we see potential in them. If we really don't understand what they go through day to day, what their life is like, what their activities are, they may never fulfill that potential. It's really important, if you want to be an asset in someone's life, to take the time to listen to him and then offer some suggestions that he may end up using down the line or even right at the moment.

How Listening Helps Us Ask Better Questions

Dr. Linda Darling-Hammond emphasizes the importance of good inquiry in any learning situation:

We're not doing what Stephen Covey said: "Seek first to understand and then to be understood." I think part of good listening comes from starting with questions rather than answers. Whether you're going into a conversation in your family or you're in a formal learning situation, you need to help children and adults learn how to ask questions to advance their understanding.

We're very focused on answers. Here's the problem or the test item or whatever, what's the answer? We do much less support for inquiring with questions. A big part of any type of education is learning to ask questions, to listen for answers, to figure out how to inquire and look for evidence, and to then weigh and balance all that information, seeking additional input to come to reasoned conclusions and ways of looking at the world. That's one of the things we can do in schools: we can really organize some of the work in schools around questioning.

If you think about the human experience, questioning is what human beings have done from the beginning. Every single thing we have discovered and invented, whether it was how to make fire or the fact that if you drop certain raw foods in the fire they come out tasting better—I don't know who figured out fried and sautéed foods—all of that came from human inquiry, investigation, looking for answers, and inventing. You look around us at all that human beings have created in this world—all the things we now need to be smart enough to preserve in the decades ahead so that there is a human race and there is a planet—all of that came from questioning. That's what we're good at. We need to bring that into the way we educate and the way we communicate with one another.

How Good Listening Makes Others Feel

Life coach Simon Alexander Ong shares a wonderful story about what feeling heard can mean to people:

I read a story where there were two British Prime Ministers. And one person had the opportunity to speak to both Prime Ministers during her lifetime. She said, "I remember I spoke to the first Prime Minister and when I had a conversation with him, I felt he was the most fascinating, interesting person I'd ever met. But when I met the second Prime Minister, he made me feel *I* was the most interesting and amazing person in the world!"

And this was purely because the second Prime Minister put the focus on her. I think that it helps, when we're listening, to take away the element of judging. Because when we listen to what someone says and we judge, we're focusing on us, on our thoughts, on our model of the words, on our mentor models of the words. But when we listen with curiosity, we listen, and we want to find out more. That allows someone to be truly heard and to be truly understood.

If we come from a place of curiosity, the judging goes away without us even realizing it. Because we are saying, "Tell me more! What makes you think that? What do you mean specifically by this?" We start to really enter the other's world and that, I think, is quite powerful, not just for the listener but for the person being listened to. How often do we feel we've truly been listened to?

Do You Want to Hear It?

The 2017 Edelman Trust Barometer revealed that people are four times more likely to ignore information that supports a position they don't believe in. Soon after the results were announced, I spoke with Dr. Darling-Hammond about listening and hearing, and my question to her was, how do we get better at hearing messages we might be predisposed to ignore? How do we teach ourselves as a society to be more open, to listen more, and to respect other people's opinions, because we can have all the collaboration in the world, but if we're not willing to understand other viewpoints, we're not going to be particularly effective. Dr. Darling-Hammond weighs in:

I think we've lost ground in a couple of ways, if you look at society as a whole. One is that media now is very, very bifurcated, so if you watch MSNBC or you watch Fox News, or wherever, you get a particular way of looking at the world. There used to be, in our federal policies, something called the Fairness Doctrine. If you think back to Walter Cronkite or some of the old anchors on the news, the idea was that you would present evidence on both sides of the issue, you would let people see the evidence themselves and take it in and think about it, and you would always provide some discussion of both sides of the issue.

The Fairness Doctrine was eliminated back in the 1980s, along with some rules that required diversity of media ownership, so now our media are owned by a very small number of people and are not at all subject to a fairness doctrine. We're getting a kind of discourse that is very narrow, and that is not helping people learn to listen to one another and then think about the pros and cons.

The other thing is that, during the No Child Left Behind era in schools, federal law drove us to triple testing that was federally mandated and really focused on reading and math scores. In response, a lot of schools eliminated science, social studies, civics—that part of the curriculum got squeezed way down. We lost the kind of robust expectation that kids in schools would be learning to be citizens, engaging in civic discourse and learning how to weigh and balance ideas.

The goal became about achieving these very narrow test scores on multiple-choice forms of testing, which actually cognitively asks people not to think about various interpretations and ways you might approach the question. It doesn't encourage students to think about something that's complex, because the format is saying there's one right answer, and we're going to give you five choices. You don't even have to think about what the answers might be, and your job is to choose one that someone else has predetermined for you. Frankly, that's a dangerous form of cognition if that's all you're doing day in and day out. We have to rebuild our capacity to have more critical thinking and wider discourse in schools and in society, across all the areas that we have to deal with.

Hearing Feedback

Being a good listener can be difficult enough in neutral circumstances—but it can be especially challenging when we find ourselves in a situation where we are receiving feedback. The tendency to be defensive and to not really hear what is being said can be strong, and it can be very detrimental to our personal development. VaynerMedia's Chief Heart Officer Claude Silver talks about her agency's changing relationship with feedback:

> We have not been an agency that gave a lot of feedback to one another. We're nice guys and gals, maybe. Something that I've put in front of the agency lately, however, is the fact that when we don't give feedback, we are quite frankly preventing that person's growth. Feedback is an act of caring. And we are spending a lot of time now learning how to give feedback and also learning how to receive feedback. We're asking, how do I give feedback back to my manager? How do I manage up? These are types of things that we have to get better at. We're 800 people, and people need to know how they're doing and they need to be heard.
>
> One of the things I've said before is that people need people. People need people who will listen, and people need people who will take action. My job, and senior leadership's job, is to take action. When you see something, say something. We don't want negativity. Instead, we say, let's talk about the issue at hand. Let's talk about why you didn't get a raise. Let's talk about why we let your buddy go yesterday. Let's have that conversation. Everything can be worked out, but it takes communication and it takes someone who gives a you-know-what to listen to that person.
>
> If we regard the concept of feedback as an act of caring, even generosity, it can fundamentally change the way we hear it, no matter if it's negative or positive. There's actually nothing like receiving feedback from someone who believes in you and wants to help you be even better. (It's typically why you are receiving it, because if someone has given up on you or didn't care, he or she wouldn't bother to

offer it). Seeing feedback in this light helps us listen and learn more effectively. The next time someone gives you feedback: (1) Ask for more clarity (only if you need it); (2) Say "thank you!"

Cultivating Diversity for a Range of Viewpoints

Pat Wadors joined me for the *Year of the Peer* podcast as CHRO of Linke-dIn. Today, she serves as Chief Talent Offer and CHRO at ServiceNow. During my conversation with her, she touched on the value of diversity when it comes to collaboration and teamwork.

At LinkedIn, we look at diversity as what makes you and me unique— and it's not just color of our skin. It's not our gender alone. It's how we were raised. It's where we were raised, our socioeconomic conditions. It is a whole bunch of different beliefs, learning differences, introversion/extroversion you name it. These varied pieces of the self all play a part in how you show up and solve problems and innovate solutions. If you want to cultivate a diverse workforce, you've got to make sure your pipeline is out there reaching that diverse workforce and having the right storytelling. Not only do we want you, but we want you to thrive while you're at LinkedIn.

Speak Less, Listen More

Ryan Foland regards asking questions not only as a key to better listening but also as a way to building more effective relationships:

If you're the person who just rambles on when you meet people, and you're just talk, talk, talk, talk, talk, they might not want you as part of their group because they don't have a chance to chirp in. It works in a twofold way because if you speak less, you can listen more, and if you speak less, whatever you say has greater authority. The less you say, the more profound you appear, so that's a good way to filter out people around you in conversations.

Don't be pegged as the guy who just keeps talking. Ask questions; listen. There's a really great study where a series of individuals are talking to each other, and they're meeting for the first time. The researchers survey participants after the fact, and the people who thought they were the most connected were the ones who talked the most and the people who didn't talk as much weren't connected as much. So, if you want people to feel connected with you, let them talk.

There's a lot of research around this point as it relates to job interviews. The idea is that, even when you are the interviewee, you should ask good questions and really listen, because the person who speaks the most is the one who usually thinks the conversation went the best. What you want is for the employer to feel that way.

Foland also shared a sentiment that's been voiced repeatedly by leadership expert Ken Blanchard. Blanchard, who's written more than fifty books, most of which have been co-authored, is often asked, "Why did you co-author so many books?" And he says, "Because I know what I know. I want to work on something with someone where I get to learn what they know."

Curiosity Doesn't Kill the Cat, After All

Asking good questions is often driven by our level of curiosity. Tim Sanders, former Chief Solutions Officer for Yahoo!, offered his perspective on the value of being curious when it comes to listening and learning:

Heed the belief of the late Sam Walton, who said, "Curiosity doesn't kill the cat. It kills the competition." As a leader, be more curious and less reactive. When someone has an opinion that's different from yours, look at it as a learning opportunity. Seek to understand what's behind it. The most important command a leader can give these days is the following three words: Tell me more. If you really want to learn what's coming next, you have to grasp the things that bug you most.

I'll give you a starting point for those of you who may be in your fifties or sixties: I want you to think differently about millennials. We tend to talk about "millennials" like it's a bad word. They're different. They are as different as the baby boomers were to the greatest generation, which did not understand them either. But somehow, the greatest generation understood that the boomers had a skillset and a value set that was the future, and it's time for us to make that same decision.

We, as leaders, need to embrace them for the reasons they are different, understanding that generational cohorts aren't about values. They are about context. "Where were you when you were eleven?" That determines your generational attitude. The millennials were raised online. They were raised in a world of school shootings, 9/11, Hurricane Katrina, where they understand to their bones that they don't have much time. That's why they're impatient. They can't really depend on anything, from an organizational standpoint. That's why they move around a lot in their employment life. Most importantly, they can't succeed without the kindness of strangers. This is why they're so good at building teams and working as tribes in communities. If we as leaders would try to learn from them and let them mentor us, not only would we create a better environment for their success, we would learn so much about how to maintain our relevance well into our seventies and eighties.

Affirmation or Exploration?

Sam Reese is the CEO of Vistage Worldwide, an organization that assembles and facilitates peer groups for CEOs and business leaders across the globe. Reese believes that our ability to listen and learn often depends on whether we tend to listen for affirmation or for exploration. For example, are we just trying to take in information that bolsters our own beliefs or are we open to expanding our worldview?

> We're all in the business of making decisions. We all seek advice from people, and this is where Vistage can change your lens: what we often don't realize is that we go to get advice from people whose reaction we already know. We do it because we just want affirmation. We ask, "Am I right or am I wrong?" Then when the other person agrees, we say, "Oh, yeah, we made a great decision here."
>
> That is where Vistage helps. Through peer groups, I became a better listener to people who provide advice because they actually know who I am, how I think, and had taken time to understand me and my concerns. Before, as a leader, when people would give me advice, I always would say to them in my head, "Yeah, but you don't know what I'm going through. You don't get this." So that's what Vistage does.
>
> It takes a while to get there because I have to open up so my group knows where I'm good, where I'm bad, my weaknesses, my strengths, where I struggle. Now, when I get advice and someone calls BS, I listen better. I think "Leo knows me, and when he's giving me this, he's got all this relationship integrity that we've built up with each other." That is what's different. The experience makes you listen differently.

Key Takeaways

One of my favorite millennials, Benji Hyam, sums up this chapter's wonderful collection of voices on the topic of listening for understanding rather nicely: "I think this is one of the biggest challenges we face in the US today. If you think about politics, laying aside for a moment the workplace, I think we've gotten to a point where people are just discarding opposing viewpoints and are not open to listening to other people's opinions and ideas. It's gotten to the point where you just kind of shrug off someone else who doesn't believe the same way you do. I think we need to have real conversations."

Real conversations are easier when we have a safe haven, an environment where we listen to learn and leave our judgments of others and their ideas at the door. Let's take a peek at what that looks like.

CHAPTER 7

Communication and the Power of the Safe Haven

To make a long (and painful) story short, I was on the track team for one year in junior high school. Typically, I ran the mile, but at the last meet of the season I was also asked to fill in as the third leg on our undefeated one-mile relay team. No problem, I thought. I had practiced the relay many times and was looking forward to contributing however I could. I ran the third leg, starting slightly back in second place. By the time I was ready to pass the baton, I had taken the lead. Our anchor leg was the fastest kid in the city. No way we could lose. As I was passing the baton, I felt a brief moment of excitement … until the baton hit the ground. So much for our undefeated season.

I was devastated, and I don't think the members of that relay team have spoken to me since. After the race, I was searching for answers as to how this could have happened. The coach wasn't bashful about offering me some clarity, stating in no uncertain terms that the loss was my fault. "You should never let go of the baton until you're certain the receiver has grasped it," he told me.

One of the first times I shared this "not my finest moment" story I was with one of my peer groups, and, interestingly enough, my failure gave permission to others to share their own similar stories. Sharing these stories reminded us not only that we're not alone—we have all experienced moments we'd love to have back—but that talking about our failures can drive deeper conversations about lessons learned.

In my case, I was challenged to look at dropping the baton as a metaphor for learning an important lesson. The more the group talked, the more we explored my story's relevance to communication. Like it or not, we concluded, the responsibility for delivering a message falls on the sender, not the receiver. You can't just say, "It was in the e-mail" or, "Sure, it's right there in paragraph 8." If you want to be a good leader/communicator, you have to accept the responsibility that comes with it. You should never let go of the baton (message) until you know that the recipients have received and thoroughly understand it. Only at that point can you relax and let them run with it.

Again, I'd give anything to have that moment back so I could pass the baton to my teammate flawlessly and watch him sprint to victory. Since I can't have a do-over, I now take solace in the fact that dropping the baton that day, and having a group with whom I could share my failure (as long ago as it may have been), provided me the most powerful leadership communication lesson of my life. Remember Sekou Andrews's powerful observation: "You win some, you learn some."

Why Safe Havens Can Help You Win and Learn More Often

For most of us, there are few places we can regard as safe havens, places where we can truly be ourselves, away from the pressure of always putting our best face forward. We all need places where we can admit we screwed up and where others can help us create value out of failure.

One of the advantages of a professional peer advisory group is that it provides a safe haven for CEOs and business leaders. By safe haven, I mean that group members feel they are in a place where they are free to share their deepest thoughts and feelings about their private lives or their businesses without fear of being judged, and where confidentiality is sacrosanct. What happens in the room stays in the room.

The interesting part, though, is that not everyone chooses to take advantage of this safe place. This was among the most interesting findings from the roughly forty workshops I conducted for CEOs and business leaders since the spring of 2016.

Before I share my findings about safe havens, let me take a moment to describe the workshop. Developed as a self-assessment tool for peer advisory groups, the workshop focuses on the five factors common to high-performing peer groups as outlined in *The Power of Peers*. These factors are (1) Having the right people in the group; (2) promoting a safe and confidential environment; (3) fostering valuable interaction; (4) enjoying a culture of member-to-member accountability; and (5) having a servant leader who serves as the steward of the other four factors.

The program is divided into three segments. In segment 1, I deliver a presentation about the five factors and detail how and why high-performing peer advisory groups are so effective. This presentation sets the stage for the workshop.

In segment 2, I stop talking, and the group begins its work. I divide the large group into small groups, where they engage in conversations about what each factor means to them and define it in terms of an ideal state. As a group they then rank themselves, using a scale of 1–10, based on their own definition of the ideal, and they identify what it would take to go from their current ranking to where they'd like to be in six months to a year. Looking at the first factor, for example, "having the right people in the group" is going to mean different things for different groups, depending upon what they believe would maximize member/group value. Members in a group of eight may decide that everyone would benefit if the group were larger, and may set a goal of expanding to twelve members. They would also identify the attributes of the four new members, deciding what qualities would best round out the group. They would follow a similar process for the remaining four factors.

In segment 3, members develop an action plan that gets them to their goal; if they've decided to expand their group from eight to twelve, for example, they create a plan for recruiting the four members with the desirable attributes they've identified. The group forms a plan for improving upon each of the five factors, including providing invaluable feedback to the group leader. At the end of the workshop, the group members not only have a peer group action plan, they receive a deck that walks them through the process of leading a similar exercise with teams back at their companies in an effort to make them higher performing as well.

Safe Haven Findings

Throughout the workshops, groups' ratings of their current status against what they define as ideal varied greatly among the factors, with one exception. On a scale of 1–10, group members consistently scored their group's success in promoting a safe and confidential environment between 9 and 10. Without fail, the members touted the judgment-free environment and their complete trust that what they discussed stayed in the room.

After leading about ten of these workshops, I asked members to give me a second ranking for this factor: I asked, "How well do you, as members, take full advantage of this safe haven?" When I posed this question, the ranking dropped for just about every group, often to a 5 or 6. It's hard not to applaud their honesty.

Just because group members say the environment is safe doesn't mean they're willing to share all of their thoughts, feelings, and challenges with the group. It's a little like being near a beautiful swimming pool on a hot day. You know the water is perfect and would feel great if you got in. Yet rather than go for a swim, you either stay in the lounge chair or just stick your toes in the water, neither of which will help you experience the cooling benefits that come with total immersion. While sharing freely with the group may not be easy, those who want to maximize their return on investment from their peer group fearlessly jump in. They realize that the more they give, the more they receive.

How a Safe Haven Worked for Carol Tometsko

Carol Tometsko is the Chief Executive Officer and President of Litron Laboratories, which she co-founded in 1976 with her late husband, Dr. Andrew M. Tometsko. Starting the company had been her husband's dream. Andrew and Carol both worked at the National Lab in Brookhaven on Long Island. Carol quit her job to complete her undergraduate degree, and then she and her husband moved from Long Island to Rochester in 1966 with their six-week-old son, Drew. For the next ten years, Andrew taught and conducted research at the University of Rochester Medical Center in biochemistry, and Carol was a stay-at-home mom earning her graduate degree in the evenings.

One day, Andrew came home from the university and said, "What do you think about starting our own business?" Carol couldn't believe her ears. Andrew loved research and teaching, but the politics of academic life just didn't suit him. She knew he was frustrated in his work, so when he said, "Let's do this thing," she went to her aerobics class, parked on the side of the road on her way home, had a good cry, walked in the door, and said, "Sure, let's do it."

Fast-forward eighteen years, and their company, Litron Laboratories, was still in business, largely because they were extremely successful in obtaining government grants. Then, in 1994, Carol was at the airport when she received a call that Andrew had passed away suddenly. She went back to the lab to find two employees who were as grief-stricken as she was, and in that moment, she decided to continue to run the business. At this point in her life Carol was still wearing a scientist's hat, and did not consider herself a businessperson. While she thought about hiring outside leadership to take the helm, she did not.

By this time, Litron had developed a kit for the Ames test, which is one of many genetic toxicology tests that have to be run before a new drug, chemical, or medical device can enter the marketplace. Other scientists at the time were saying, "You know, kits are the way to go because, in this day and age, nobody wants to take chemicals off the shelf for fear of contamination." In 1995, Litron began developing and selling kits, but Carol understood that she couldn't build a company based on that approach alone. Carol told me, "We had to get involved in new areas, in exploring new genetic toxicology areas. That's where we sort of were stumped."

In 1997, Tom Merkel, a personal friend of Carol's, suggested she join a CEO peer advisory group. Carol asserts that it was her group members who taught her the word "collaboration." Until that time, she'd lived in a world where scientist was pitted against scientist in a race to arrive at the answer first, so she found the idea of collaborating with other scientists somewhat frightening, though an intriguing idea for scaling her business. Carol's main scientist, Steve Dertinger, agreed. Without the safe haven Carol experienced as a peer advisory group member, it's unlikely she would have created a group for scientists. Eighteen years later, Carol is still a member of her CEO peer advisory group, and Litron is an internationally renowned entity built on peer relationships, both with her group members and with scientists the world over.

Being Open Is an Act of Generosity and Courage

Being truly open about feelings, ideas, and possibilities requires a bit of retraining for most of us. In Chapter 2, Brian Mac Mahon talked about his son's fearless nature, and how it was only a matter of time before it would be beaten out of him. I recall a story from my own childhood that underlines this point. An elementary school teacher asserted that life on other planets wasn't possible because of a lack of oxygen, and I raised my hand and asked, "What if other life forms could survive by breathing something else? Why couldn't there be some little kid out there breathing nitrogen?" If the teacher didn't call me an idiot directly, she sure made me feel like one.

You can imagine the hesitation I felt over raising my hand again to share an "out of the box" comment. Today, I realize that I wasn't the idiot that day. I also learned, over time, that giving of ourselves to others is an act of generosity as well as one of courage. Sharing our perspective is a generous gift to others—it will either open their minds to something new or solidify their current beliefs. It's an act of courage because most of us have endured experiences like the one I shared, and being vulnerable again in that way is no small act.

Leadership and Courage— and Modeling the Way

I had the honor of spending some time in Boston with former CEO of Ford Motor Company Alan Mulally. Mulally's tenure as CEO is widely heralded, and during his early months at Ford, he had some work to do to create an environment in which the senior leadership team felt empowered to raise their hands and admit they had a problem or challenge with which they needed help. As the story goes, Alan led a regular meeting with his senior leaders in which they reported on their dashboards. They would report green if they were on track, while yellow signaled a caution, and red was trouble. Ford was losing $17 billion at the time, and as Alan called on the leaders to share their dashboards, they all were showing green(s) across the board. Imagine being the CEO, taking charge of a company that's losing $17 billion, and getting feedback from your senior leaders that everything in the field is going great. Could there be worse news?

You see, the culture at Ford was one that did not permit anyone to publicly admit to problems or challenges. As much as Alan encouraged someone, anyone, to step up and share his challenges, the leaders didn't trust that it was okay to do so. Finally, one executive raised his hand and said, "Hey, I've got an issue over here." Alan stood up and applauded this leader, and they all addressed the concern. Over time, the CEO was able to create an environment of safety, in which people were willing to share and work together—and this was no small reason that Ford performed as well as it did in the coming years.

For me, the most wonderful part of this story is that the very first person who had the courage to admit a problem succeeded Mulally as CEO of Ford. It's worth noting that Mulally's ability to create a safe environment and to build and foster a new culture was instrumental to fueling Ford's turnaround.

Jim Kouzes, co-author of *The Leadership Challenge*, responded to the Ford story this way: "It's a wonderful story. It illustrates how important it is for senior executives to model the behavior that they expect from others. In this case, they modeled behavior of always being curious, always admitting that you don't know everything, and being willing to ask for help from other people."

Putting Our Best Face Forward

Imagine for a moment that you didn't have to be on stage all the time—which is often how we feel, right? We try to be the best version of ourselves, which means we don't always feel we can (or should) be our authentic selves in many situations in life. The thing is, when everyone does that, and when we take other people's personas at face value, we may look at our own lives rather critically because we tend to compare everything we know about ourselves with the highlight reel others are sharing about their lives. During an episode of *Year of the Peer*, Thais Sky talked about putting our best face forward:

I've seen a culture video online about having to put on a face. In Japan, that's just as true as in the Western world, so they created a mask you can put on your face that's a smile, so you don't have to put on a face, so that everyone will think you're smiling. It's a joke. It's a parody. It plays into the very real dilemma we all have, which is not being authentically ourselves in the world. It's exhausting. Putting ourselves up on this pedestal and having to pretend that we're better than people and that we have it all together is exhausting. It's the way we've been conditioned. For many, many years, we have to pretend that everything is good in order to be seen as professional, as someone you'd want to do business with.

I find that it's the people who are most real with me who I want to work with. If they're real with me now, they're going to be real with me if the project isn't working. They're going to be real with me if their time-line isn't working. They're going to be more likely to call me out on my stuff. That's the type of people I want to work with. If I'm hiring a copywriter, I want her to say, I don't think this is a good program, and here's why. If they're not willing to even let me know how they feel, how do I know that they're going to be willing to let me know what's real in my business?

Sharing Experiences Rather Than Advice Promotes a Safe Haven

Safe havens are places where we are free to be our authentic selves. Young President's Organization (YPO) CEO Scott Mordell shares his thoughts on how YPO's member-led forums create the kind of common ground that makes safe havens possible, because members share experiences rather than give advice:

Sometimes people say, "Look, I'm stuck, and I just want somebody to give me some advice. I know it's coming from a good place, but just, what should I do?" Of course, advice makes things less safe. Because if you were to give me advice I hadn't solicited, and you said, "Scott, never wear a blue shirt on a podcast, you look like an idiot," now I'm feeling like I'm being judged. And as soon as I'm being judged or I'm not wanting to follow your advice, I (1) do not want to disappoint you; (2) don't want or like to be judged; and (3) am feeling like, "Oh, now I've got conflicting advice, and I'm gonna make somebody unhappy with my choice."

Now I'm thinking about my reaction to the people who gave me advice more than I'm thinking about my own particular situation. So, we have in our forum protocols to avoid giving advice. We say, "Don't 'should' on anybody, okay? 'You should.' Don't 'should' on anybody," because once you're beginning to give advice, you're making the whole dialogue a little bit less safe. We've taken that over the years since YPO was founded and made a recommendation that the best way to react to somebody's situation is not to say, "Hey, that's really interesting, Leo, have you thought about this, this, or that?" It's really to say, "That's really interesting, Leo, I had a very similar thing and here's what I went through." And I walk through my particular situation and then somebody else does the same, and pretty soon we are all reflecting on our own situations instead of trying to solve one person's issue.

So, once we don't give advice and we all participate in sharing experiences; now, the question that one had is actually the same question and issue that eight are working through, but from different angles. And then when you wrap that up, you actually get more powerful feedback and conclusions, and the person who had the original issue has much more that she can walk out of the room with and really carry with her.

Circles CEO Dan Hoffman adds,

Susan Cain wrote *Quiet: The Power of Introverts in a World That Can't Stop Talking*,[1] and there's been a lot of attention to this movement. I think one of the things we've discovered is that it's important to have a safe space where you know you're going to get called on and there's no small talk ... 40% of the population are introverts. It's actually a lot higher with entrepreneurs. You hate small talk, so it's like building this place where there's no small talk—"I know everyone's going to speak equally. I'm not going to have to sit there listening to someone run on"—unlocks this thing for people with an introvert profile.

Anyway, to summarize, process and the right mix of ingredients for the right case produces this experience of deep and safe space and opening up that's very powerful. It produces it fairly consistently. Some people say, "It's not my cup of tea," and that's fine. We sort of build that into the model. Some people don't realize that's what's happening.

Key Takeaways

In building deep, meaningful, and mutually beneficial relationships with a diverse group of people, we tend to listen, learn, and grow in ways we could never do alone or without people who push us out of our comfort zone from time to time. The stories and concepts shared by leaders from various walks of life all have a common theme, one that aligns with Samuel Clemens' assertion that we have one mouth and two ears for a reason.

Reference

1. Cain, Susan. *Quiet: The Power of Introverts in a World That Can't Stop Talking.* New York, NY: Random House, 2013.

CHAPTER 8

Good Givers Are Great Getters

More than twenty years ago, much to the chagrin of many agency principals and Human Resources professionals at the time, I wrote an article for *Inside PR* describing my interviewing policy.[1] I share this not because I'm comfortable calling myself generous but because it's a strong illustration of the many benefits, some of which were quite unexpected, that came to me and my firm because of a simple promise I made to myself in the early 1990s. Here's the story as I shared it in the article[1]:

WHY WE INTERVIEW ANYONE WHO ASKS

In the fall of 1990, as the real estate market in New England foundered, I found myself without a job. I was laid off my position as director of public relations for a major real estate development corporation, and along with many in those days, found myself looking for work. At the time, I was relatively self-assured about my background and experience. I had a good resume, strong portfolio, and several byline articles that I had written for various PR and industry trade books. I believed if I could just meet the employers face to face, then I could make a strong case for being hired. I responded to ads, followed up with phone calls, talked to recruiters, and exhausted my contacts. The competitive environment for communications positions was brutal. My greatest frustration was that I found securing actual face-to-face interviews next to impossible. It was six months before I actually found a job. Enough time to understand the feeling that comes from watching the business world function perfectly well without my personal involvement. I think I had three interviews during my entire search. I promised myself that if the tables were ever turned, I would do whatever I could to give job applicants the opportunity to present themselves in person.

Fortunately, the tables did turn, and since 1992 I have been in the position to hire people. Today, we interview any person who calls our company seeking one. Whenever I make that statement to people, their first reaction is: "How on earth do you have time?" What started out as a mission to keep a personal promise has turned into one of the most valuable initiatives for our organization. As a result, we make the time.

Here are the (major outcomes) reasons for our interview policy:

- It keeps us informed of all the talent available in our market. Situations can change quickly. It keeps us a step ahead, whether we need to fill a permanent position or find a specialist for a short-term assignment.

- It's consistent with our mission of serving as a public relations resource. We want to be a PR resource for everyone; we don't discriminate against job applicants.
- Every person I've hired since 1992 has been as a result of this process. No advertising costs. No executive recruitment fees.
- Major corporations and other organizations in the area are aware of our policy. We receive calls frequently asking for recommendations and resumes. (Remember our "PR Resource" mission?)
- It sharpens the interview skills of all our employees who participate.
- It's proven to be great PR for our firm.
- It's the right thing to do. We've all been on the other side of the desk.
- (And here's one of the most unexpected outcomes)
- These applicants eventually get jobs. Not necessarily with us of course, but better still, companies that can hire us. Individuals who've remembered that we gave them the time when others wouldn't have rewarded us on numerous occasions.

While this process may still seem frightening to some, it's well worth it. We are continually delighted by the quality of people we meet and the level of talented PR professionals residing in our community. As for me, I'm grateful for every day that I have an office from which to work.

The Influence of Affluence

Lewis Schiff, executive director of the Business Owners Council, and co-founder (with Norm Brodsky) of Birthing of Giants, talks about the difference between those people who emerge from their middle-class roots and those who do not:

The Business Owners Council is a real-world experiment of research I did in 2005 for a book called *The Influence of Affluence*.[2] In that book, we looked at 3000 people who started out life in the middle class and remained in the middle class throughout their money-earning years. We also studied about 700 people who had started out middle class and became very successful .... We asked them all the same questions and we compared the differences. How do 700 people emerge out of the middle class, while most of us stay in the group we started in? One of the four most important answers concerned the ways they managed relationships. We call it networking, which is a very simple word and which means different things to different people. You can call it mentorship or you can call it networking—it really has to do with how you decide to interact with another person.

What I did with the Business Owners Council after the research I'd done is I worked with *Inc.* magazine, one of the great, great magazines that cover entrepreneurship, and I asked them to help me create a group of people who, if they were in the room together, would know how to give a lot to each other. These are people who would understand, as all self-made people in America do, that you have to be a giver in order to be a getter, in business terms. It wasn't hard. We put a lot of high-performing business owners in the room and they looked around the room and they looked around the room and then identified a person, or two, or five. They would go to that person and they'd say, "Who are you? What are you about? What's important to you?" Then they would follow up with leads, with ideas, with solutions. They were helping, with the basic understanding that you must give to the right groups of people in order to get a lot in return. That's the energy, the business model, behind the Business Owners Council that I run today.

On Love and Mentoring

Former Yahoo! Chief Solutions Officer and best-selling author Tim Sanders emphasizes love and mentoring and the difference they can make to our success:

I'm a guy from a farming community in eastern New Mexico, right on the border of West Texas. I was raised by my grandmother. I took all of my childhood experiences and poured them into a game-changing opportunity in the mid-1990s, when I had a chance to go to work for Mark Cuban at Broadcast.com. At the time, the company was called AudioNet. The name of the company changed later, but Cuban was an amazing influence, not just on me but on everybody who worked with him at the time.

He believed that the secret to success is to make love, not war. Find out what the customer wants and give it to them without any objection. He believed that the future was in books. He got me on a tear, and I became a voracious reader and a dedicated student of the game because he believed that, in times of great change, we can add a lot of value to our colleagues and customers by having something valuable to share, especially insights, complex solutions to complex problems.

So during that time with Cuban I really began to try out this new theory I had. The theory was something I'd been raised on, communicated by people like a Zig Ziglar, or a Norman Vincent Peale, or even Napoleon Hill—and it is old school. I had this idea that if you promote other people's success and all you expect from them is for them to seize the opportunity and pay it forward, you will build an outstanding brand. You'll put yourself around the right kind of people, and when you achieve your own success, which you will, you'll look back on it later in your career, as I'm doing now, and you'll enjoy the whole thing a second time.

I wanted to become a successful person, and I knew I had to become a specific type of businessperson to become successful. One businessperson I admired, who was highly successful because of his generosity, was not a person to be taken lightly. I'm referring to Herb Kelleher, founder of Southwest Airlines. Someone had referred to him as a tough old love cat, and that's where everything clicked.

Here's the idea. Nice, smart people succeed. Do not forget the second word, *smart*. Herb Kelleher succeeded not only because he was generous but because he understood that love requires technique, especially at work. What I mean by this is that, in the professional sense, when you love somebody you will share your intangibles with them—your knowledge and your network and your compassion—to promote their success. You have an emotional feeling about them. It's called caring, and you want to share something with them.

You want them to avoid the unnecessary suffering in their business lives, and that's what I see people like Herb and a lot of other people I've met over the last twenty years doing, but you have to keep improving your giving technique so you pick the right heroes, help them in a way that they act on, and mentor them to pay it forward. And you have to learn to manage your ego when the occasional person doesn't thank you, doesn't show gratitude, doesn't give you anything in return, though I don't expect it. Or, in some cases, the person may take your advice, run with it, and later compete with you. That's a real challenge over the course of a career, to deal with what I call ego economics.

Why Mentoring Matters

Tim Sanders notes that being a mentor means serving as a humble teacher:

We should always be mentoring people. It's one thing for me to give you a couple of tips, like, "Hey, this is the kind of web com I use," or whatever. That's a tip. That's a technique. While that's valuable and brings return on attention to a conversation, mentorship is a commitment. Mentorship is me, the humble teacher, recognizing you as the hero on a journey going somewhere a little too fast. You need a teacher to give you a gift for the next stage of your journey. That's love. That's caring about a person.

I'll tell you something else, mentorship is about caring about the ecosystem you live in. You mentor the heroes so they don't crash and burn, because we need more heroes in the world we live in. So the idea here is to look for people who demonstrate heroic qualities. They've got courage. They've got a set of values that resonates with you. They have ambition. They've got pluck. But you look for that little gap in the person's insight arsenal that you think you can help with, and that's who you mentor. Don't get stuck in the Star Wars, Karate Kid, wise-old-man way of thinking about it. It's not about you at the end of your career taking some twenty-something under your wing. That's not mentorship. Mentorship is helping anyone.

In fact, if you go back to Greek mythology, mentorship's roots in Greek mythology started with lesser gods and humans giving advice to gods like Hercules. Everywhere you go, look for the hero. Don't worry about his rank versus your title. Mentor people and you'll generate incredible relationships. By the way, you just may learn something.

Paying It Forward

Jeffrey Hayzlett, best-selling author and chairman of C-Suite Network, is a big believer in the power of paying it forward, investing time and resources in the people and ideas of the future in the same way people helped him during his own journey. Hayzlett says,

I'm a real believer in the idea that I didn't get here by myself. I love the expression, "When you make it to the top, you have to remember to send the elevator back down for everybody else." And I'm a real believer in that, because the more that we can get everybody up, the more we can grow. And I've always learned that the more you give, give, give, the more you get, get, get. So I'm constantly working on helping other people and reaching out. One, because it makes you feel good. Two, because it's the right thing to do. And three, you don't get here because you did it by yourself. There were other people who helped you. I've been in business for a long, long time, and I've been real successful but I've had a lot of failures, too.

And in those failures, there were people who took care of me, meaning they could've been mean, they could've been rough, they could've crushed me, could've squeezed me at a time when it would've been a really bad thing in the end. Yet they took the initiative. So why can't I do that? Why can't I be helpful in that? I keep in touch with lots of people, constantly … I mean, I send out e-mails at 2:00 or 3:00 in the morning, or late at night. A lot of people say, "Well, Jeff, is this really you or is this an automated letter?" No. This is really me, clipping and pasting, clipping and pasting and hitting send. And I do a lot of that, because I think it makes a big difference, quite frankly.

Knowledge Sharing and Being Human

Tim Sanders looks at leading with generosity in terms of sharing knowledge and simply being human:

In *Love Is the Killer App*,[3] I say, "Having knowledge and having awareness of insights is important, but it only becomes real when you share it with someone else." Because life is about these collaborative conversations where we play with each other. Knowledge sharing, even though I think about it as bringing a gift to every conversation, is really the ultimate way to collaborate on the courage to seize our future.

In work situations I have encouraged people, "Listen, be human. Care about that person today, because I guarantee you when I see you forty-five years from now …" I used to say this a long time ago in Boca Raton and we're shuffling around, we're not going to talk about what we accumulated or titles on business cards. We're going to talk about those wonderful people that we did time with at IBM, and we're not going to think back on them dispassionately. We may have, in the moment, to protect ourselves. I say, much like Stephen Covey, "Seeing your road, it changed my life. Start with the end in mind." Because that's what compassion is. It is recognizing that the only thing you love to do is be alive with other humans. So do it at work.

Here is how I apply this: I let compassion become the center of the way I design solutions and react to other people, because everything we do at work is either a design issue or a reaction issue. In conversations, when we react to each other, do we do it with compassion? Am I thinking about that as I react to you? Is empathy part of my toolkit? Because, I'm telling you, empathy is a super power for leaders, and few possess it. When I'm trying to solve a problem, whether I'm thinking about the structure of my company or a new product or a new marketing plan or a new compensation scheme, I ask myself: Have I put compassion at the center of the table?

You say, "Well, you can't run a business if you put solving unnecessary suffering at the center of the table." I'm like, "What about design-oriented companies like Tesla or Apple or other organizations where customer-experience design is about compassion?" The whole secret to customer-experience design is to eliminate unnecessary suffering, and whenever possible produce memorable moments of happiness. So why don't we lead like that? That's what I mean by leading with compassion.

Community

In my exchange with Brian Mac Mahon, he talks about community and peer groups, and the importance of putting yourself in a solid position to help others:

When I speak about community, it's not just about the larger companies helping the smaller companies. We've all got a currency, every one of us. I'm a big pay-it-forward guy. For me, it's about helping out, but you don't help out in a foolish way. You don't want to spend all your time helping people who get no direct benefit from what you're doing because what will happen is this: you will run out of time. And then what? You'll end up the nicest poor guy on the side of the street. It's much better to put yourself in a strong position, and then you can help as many people as you want because you're financially and fiscally responsible and strong.

What I love about peer groups is the very first word. It's *peer*. You get people who have a currency to bring to the table. And then the responsibility of everybody within the group is to help everybody else in the group. When you do it properly, it's just fabulous. I've always loved peer groups. I've always felt that such groups do a few things. Not only do they force people to think about ways that they need to help the peer before the meeting happens, but the group keeps everybody accountable because you have people around you who are not just gonna accept, "Yeah, I didn't hit my numbers. It was a bad month." Let's hope it goes well next month because a proper peer group will say, "I'm sorry, that's not good enough."

I love really serious people and I love really serious groups. I think that most of us, outside peer groups, don't take our time seriously enough. We don't weigh its value. I hear people say, "Well, it didn't cost me anything. It was just my time." Time is the only thing we have. The great thing about going into a peer group with a two-hour period or an hour-and-a-half period is that the only thing you're intending is to become successful with one another. Everybody has a hyper-focus on solving the problems that need solving so that everybody can move on to a different chasm. I love that book, *Crossing the Chasm*,[4] which talks about the different segments of challenges you have. Sometimes you just need a bunch of other people to push you a little bit so you can get past it.

Giving as Sharing

I asked Brian Mac Mahon whether he finds the peers in his groups willing and able to be open and share with one another right out of the gate, or whether that comfort is built over time. Are people willing to share at that very first meeting? How do the relationships evolve as these groups work together? Mac Mahon responded:

It's been really powerful for us. We've been blown away. I suppose impressed is better than blown away. I don't know why I naively expected everybody to want to help each other just because they're all at the same space. Early-stage entrepreneurs are slightly more challenging than later-stage entrepreneurs or even people who have a job, because if you've got a job then you're trying to go up the ladder, you're trying to make sure that you deal with the politics, and you try to make sure that you earn money. There's a kind of continuum.

Later-stage entrepreneurs are in a place where there's not huge change. With early-stage entrepreneurs, one person could be in the middle of their branding exercise, the other person is in the middle of their product fit, and the other person has just got a concept. So you have to get people who have common, aligned interests that are going to stay aligned for at least a short to a medium-term period of time.

I have five people in one of the groups who were all building a website at the same time. How great is that? That's ten eyes looking at the customer journey, the user interface, the user experience, the design, the colors, the fonts of five websites. It's gold. I mean, you would normally have to pay a bunch of money for that. Then, as they move to the next level, they move there together, and so on.

Key Takeaways

In business, as in life, the common expression that it is better to give than to receive could not be more true: when we give, we typically receive many-fold in return. We become closer to realizing all the currencies at work in our lives. Consider the cycle: reach out to others for help, be willing to help others, do the things anyone can do, realize more success, and put yourself in a position to give and receive much more effectively. Imagine an entire society of people who did the things anyone could do just a little more often. There's no limit to what we could realize in every aspect of our lives.

Tina Martini, intellectual property attorney for DLA Piper, shares some closing thoughts: "I think it's incumbent upon us, when folks enter our lives and serve such a higher purpose for us, to do the same for others. Even if it's taking a half an hour to meet with somebody who is at a crossroads, we should try to embrace those opportunities as much as we can. It's our obligation to pay it forward, and to be that for other people as well."

References

1. Bottary, Leo J. "Why we interview anyone who asks." *Inside PR*, September 15, 1997. Reprinted with permission.
2. Prince, Russ Alan, and Lewis Schiff. *The Influence of Affluence: How the New Rich Are Changing America.* New York: Broadway Books, 2009.
3. Sanders, Tim. *Love Is the Killer App: How to Win Business and Influence Friends.* Crown Business, 2003.
4. Moore, Geoffrey A. *Crossing the Chasm: Marketing and Selling Disruptive Products to Mainstream Customers.* New York: Harper Collins, 2014.

CHAPTER 9

Why Being a Good Teammate Matters

BE A GREAT TEAMMATE.
—RyanFoland.com

During my workshops for CEOs and business leaders, I talk about how the same five factors that are common to high-performing peer groups apply to high-performing teams as well. To recap the five factors as they pertain to a team, first outlined in *The Power of Peers*, they are having (1) the right people on the team; (2) a trusting environment; (3) a productive environment;

(4) a culture of accountability; and (5) a servant leader who can serve as the steward for the other four factors. In this chapter, we'll talk about the importance of having the right people on the team and what a relentless culture of accountability looks like. We'll explore two examples, one from business and one from sports, both of which place a premium on being a good teammate.

The Culture at MullenLowe

It's been nearly ten years since I worked at Boston-based advertising agency Mullen (now MullenLowe), but the experience left an indelible impression on me. It's also the closest I've come in a business setting to being part of a culture that was so unyielding in its commitment to excellence. People who enjoy the privilege of working at MullenLowe, for however long, are surrounded by colleagues who are committed to one another and to creating great work for their clients.

The agency's new logo (an octopus wearing boxing gloves) is as indicative of the company's culture as it is of the work itself. Imagine a group of talented people, from all different backgrounds and walks of life, dedicated to their craft and committed to producing award-winning advertising that drives their clients' business. Let me illustrate what that looks like based on what I experienced in my time with the agency.

The Creative Director would gather a bunch of people from various disciplines in a room to come up with ideas for a new campaign for a client or prospect. Everyone on the team shows up to the meeting well prepared regarding the client's business, competitors, market, strategy, and so on. The ideas start flying. Everyone has their boxing gloves on—not to fight against one another but to fight for the strongest idea. Eventually, something takes shape, and the bones of a campaign are displayed on a board. People look at one another and collectively celebrate their genius—only briefly, of course, because they know it's time to start from scratch and come up with another campaign. The group will repeat the process four or five times in a relentless pursuit of what former National Geographic photographer Dewitt Jones calls "another right answer."[1]

Here's the best part: on all the occasions that I participated in that exercise, the first campaign—which everyone celebrated with such great enthusiasm—didn't make the cut to show the client. It's what happens when you have a group of people who trust and respect one another enough to go to battle for the best idea. (As an aside, my tenure at Mullen was short, largely because I was at a point in my career where I'd simply taken one agency job too many. I was burned out. And if I had to guess, Mullen's CEO at the time, Joe Grimaldi, sensed it during my interview but didn't stand in the way of my being hired. I'm glad he didn't, but I wish I could have delivered more value for a longer period of time. If I were in need of a new advertising agency today, I'd hire them in a second.)

UConn Women's Basketball Team

No team at the college or professional level has been more dominant over the past twenty years than the University of Connecticut's women's basketball team. Since 1995, the program has won eleven national championships. After having won four consecutive championships (2013–2016), the team graduated three seniors who were the top three picks in the WNBA draft: Breanna Stewart, Moriah Jefferson, and Morgan Tuck. For most programs, the 2016–2017 season would have been considered a rebuilding year. Despite a punishing non-conference schedule packed with top-ranked opponents, UConn just kept winning. And winning big—by an average margin of nearly forty points per game—continuing a winning streak led by their three former stars that would stretch to 111 games.

It's true that Geno Auriemma is a Hall of Fame head coach and that UConn's program attracts the best players in the country. Yet, there's a lot of great talent out there, and they attend schools with top programs, including Notre Dame, Texas, Tennessee, South Carolina, and so on. In *The Power of Peers*, UConn Assistant Coach and former UConn All-American Shea

Ralph shared with us that, as tough as the coaches are on the players, the players are just as tough on themselves and one another. We talked a great deal about how their culture of accountability was key to setting them apart from other teams.

Consider this: HBO aired a short series on UConn's program during the team's march through the 2017 NCAA Final Four. In one of the episodes, the coaches were stranded at their homes because of a severe snowstorm. The team, which included players who had never lost a game during their college career, didn't skip practice because the coaches couldn't be there; they trudged across campus through the snow and held their own practice. Their commitment to one another to set their own standard of excellence, and their desire to get better each and every day is what sets them apart from every other program in the United States.

There's another ingredient at work here, however, and this factor begins before a player is ever actively recruited or steps onto the UConn campus. It involves finding the kind of player who can be successful in UConn's team culture. In addition to being exceptionally skilled and highly competitive, kids who get invited to become part of this program have one quality in common: they place a premium on being a good teammate.

One of the ways the coaching staff determines whether a player has this quality involves watching the way she behaves when she's *not* actually in the game. Even the best high school basketball players will get taken out of the game for a quick breather. It's that time, while the player is on the bench, that coaches watch carefully. If the player throws a towel over her head and doesn't remain actively engaged in the game, cheering on her fellow players for the brief time she's on the bench, she is not likely to get the nod to come to UConn, no matter how many points she scores while she's on the floor. This high schooler may be a great player, but she'll probably have to play college ball elsewhere.

A player's bench-time activities may sound like a small thing, but it's an indicator of something deeper—and finding talented players who are committed first and foremost to being a good teammate is tougher than you think. Being committed to your teammates and setting your own standard of excellence every time you go to practice and in every possession during a game is a centerpiece of the culture because it's embedded in the heart of every player who accepts the responsibility to play in the program. This culture is among the reasons UConn wins the way they do and why they are in a position to compete for a national championship so often.

Finally, I'd like to share an example of how coaching staff reinforces the concept that everyone has a responsibility to bring their A game to every practice and every game. This example doesn't involve basketball at all; rather, it recounts a time when the coaching staff took the players to a Broadway play. The following day at practice, the coach asked the players what they thought of the experience. As you can imagine, the young women were blown away by the quality of the amazing performances they saw. Coach Auriemma then reminded the players that the cast performed the same play the night before and the night before that—and on Wednesdays and Saturdays they perform it twice. He continued to explain that, for each audience, most theatergoers will likely see the play only that one time. The cast realizes that, and they accept the responsibility to make it an amazing experience for that audience (every audience), no matter how many times the performers have or will put on the show.

When fans come to watch UConn play basketball, Auriemma noted, "UConn doesn't just owe fans a victory, the team wants their fans to walk out of the building having given them an experience they'll never forget." Imagine if we all showed up to work every day as if we were on stage, as if we were committed to making sure that everyone with whom we interacted saw our A game and believed they were in the presence of something special.

We're Capable of Achieving More Together

Exceptional advertising at MullenLowe and national championships at UConn are created by teams of selfless individuals who understand the concept of abundance. They know that the whole is greater than the sum of its parts. When I explained MullenLowe's culture to VaynerMedia's Chief

Heart Officer Claude Silver, this is how she responded: "I love what you just said. Everyone in that room can declare victory and feel proud to have been part of that process. And what that means is *collaboration* and *team* and *we versus I*. I've been in agencies for so long because I am not creative. I love to be around creatives. I'm a strategist. I think through stories and ideas, but I could never put pen to paper and draw or come up with a pie-in-the-sky creation, and that's the draw of being at an agency for me."

Peter Carrington, owner of the Saint Louis Barge, a floating hotel that provides an unparalleled tour of the Bordeaux region through its web of canals, says that this level of collaboration and commitment to excellence is no different in his business:

> Getting the right people on the team is about surrounding ourselves with the quality that we need. That extends beyond just the people who directly engage with our guests; it extends to the people who support the barge behind the scenes, the plumbers, the tilers, the electricians, the welders, the fuel providers. All of those people must be fit for purpose, they've got to be able to respond quickly, and they've got to know us well enough to do the work we need. If we have a pump that doesn't work I need to know the plumber will arrive as soon as he can, normally within two hours, and fix it. It's not good having some plumber who can see you next Tuesday, if your pump's not working on Wednesday. We need to keep the business functioning, we need to keep the thing rolling, and it needs to be seamless.
>
> We're very, very fortunate that we have, over the last four years, made the connections and settled on the providers of the services— the providers of the wine, the providers of the food. They know they can rely on our business, and in return we know we can rely on their support. We've made a deliberate decision to go that way. We don't look for the cheapest people, we look for the people who are the most reliable, and the best, so that we can run the business at the level it needs to run and not be casting around trying to find somebody to do something on the cheap. We're not interested in that.

How to Achieve Team and Group Accountability

When you consider everything it takes to build a program like the one at UConn, construct and develop a workplace culture like MullenLowe (or VaynerMedia), deliver the guest experience one receives on the Saint Louis, or create the onstage magic of a Broadway play, it's a wonder outstanding experiences like these ever happen.

In my workshops for CEOs and business leaders, we talk about how the leader may set the tone, but by definition, he or she can't create a workplace culture of accountability without having the right people. UConn's culture of accountability would fall apart quickly if the program moved away from the practice of recruiting good teammates. Mullen's work would suffer if the end product or the "work" became secondary to the needs and wants of individual employees. Recognizing this, we talk about a powerful leadership concept in which—when it comes to developing and sustaining a culture of accountability—the leader is not an enforcer so much as a backstop.

The Mindset of the Leader

In *The Power of Peers*, we talked about group and team leadership using a servant leadership model rather than an authoritarian model. It was our assertion that the leader is a part of the group or team, not apart from it. This model sees the leader, the group, and its individual members as equally responsible for the group's culture of accountability, relationship, communication, productivity, or growth—whatever term you want to place in the middle of the triad. Over the course of the workshops I've conducted since the release of *The Power of Peers*, I've paid special attention to group member-to-member accountability because groups or teams who enjoy this dynamic as part of their culture tend to be higher performing—witness the results of UConn women's basketball and MullenLowe (Figure 9.1).

Figure 9.1   *The peer group accountability model.*

The Mindset of the Individual and the Group

To step back for a moment, group or team accountability speaks to the way employees or members hold one another to account. Being accountable to the leader or coach is secondary. The true currency of the individuals rests with how much they trust one another to do what they say they will do without question. So what role can the leader play here?

If leaders served as enforcers, they would attempt to impose their will. Instead, they lead by teaching others that, in being accountable to one another, they can achieve true abundance. One of the greatest examples of leading by showing and teaching others can be found in the creation and implementation of the role of Walmart greeter.

The idea didn't come from senior management or from a national retail consulting firm, it came from store manager Dan McAllister of Crowley, Louisiana, who was having trouble with store theft. McAllister wanted to deter criminals yet send a positive message to his honest customers. Rather than hire a guard to stand by the door, he established a greeter program.

Sam Walton and Tom Coughlin (Senior VP, Sam's Clubs) discovered the manager's solution during a store visit. While at first they were perplexed, the manager quickly explained the reason, and the Walmart greeter program was born.

It's worth noting that, while Sam Walton loved the idea, he knew he'd have to do some convincing. Walton understood that, in order to implement such a program successfully and consistently throughout his stores, he'd have to sell store managers on the idea. The genius and patience of Sam Walton were evident in the fact that it took about eighteen months for him to convince his managers and get the greeter program up and running in all of Walmart's stores.

Whether you're a business leader, a coach, or a parent, the members on your team have to come to their own understanding and beliefs. When they do this, true team alignment becomes possible.

The enforcement model of accountability is shown in Figure 9.2. Leaders who play the role of backstop tend to see the model as shown in Figure 9.3.

When I lead workshops with CEO peer groups, I ask the group members to rank their culture of accountability to one another on a scale of 1–10, based on how they hold one another accountable for what members say they will do both inside and outside the meeting. Too often, members admit that on a scale of 1–10 their culture of accountability rests somewhere between 4 and 6. They understand that if they had a stronger culture of accountability, the group would be exponentially stronger.

Figure 9.2   *Group accountability model—enforcement.*

Figure 9.3   *Group accountability model—backstop.*

When asked how they could improve, members often provide suggestions for how the leader of the group can "enforce" this culture. It doesn't take long, however, for one of the members to say, "Wait a minute, creating a culture of group accountability isn't up to the leader, it's up to us!" After group members offer suggestions for often-complex systems that could be put into place, I suggest that encouraging accountability may be about adopting a different mindset.

Here's one way to illustrate the point: If I'm a member of the group and I raise an issue or opportunity with which I would like their help, we may spend thirty to forty-five minutes talking about it. At the end, I'll let the group know which ideas and experiences resonated with me and share what I plan to do with those ideas by the time we get together for our next meeting. At the next meeting, using the backstop model, it would be my responsibility to report my progress back to the group. I shouldn't wait to be asked. After all, they spent their time and shared their wisdom and experiences to equip me to make a better decision. The least I can do is express my gratitude by letting them know how their input helped me. Every member of the group should consider it their personal responsibility to act accordingly.

The next line of defense, using this model, is expecting the group to emphasize accountability, not the leader. In the event I came to the next meeting and either wanted to avoid the conversation because I had not done what I said I would do or simply had fifty other things on my mind and forgot to report back to the group, the leader of the group would wait for one of the members to say, "Hey, Leo, tell us how's it going with that challenge you posed to us last month." Again, the dynamic reinforces being accountable to the other group members, not the leader. Of course, in the unlikely event that I didn't bring it up, and not one member of the group asked me, the leader would step in, reminding me and the group of our respective responsibilities. This is how the group learns.

Key Takeaways

Simon Alexander Ong's passion for Mastermind groups, which began when he was a young boy and grabbed Napoleon Hill's *Think and Grow Rich*[2] off the bookshelf, is palpable:

> Being held accountable to a group of people who are committed, that's the key part for me. Over time, by consciously changing who I surrounded myself with, I began to understand the difference between commitment and interest. Because people who are simply interested talk about things more than they actually do them. But I found that people who are committed have eliminated excuses. They've made a decision that this is going to happen, no matter what. They've made up their minds, and the focus now is on how to make things happen. That mindset shift was very powerful for me to experience.

Etienne Wenger-Trayner adds, "People have to know who is a good learning partner because they share an interest, they share a need to learn about something that's in common, otherwise it's just a conversation over a beer. It's fine, but if you want to really make progress, you need to make sure that the person you're talking to has some appreciation for the challenge, and understands why it's important to learn how to solve it, and sees that they can apply it in their own practice."

References

1. DewittJones. Accessed November 26, 2017. http://dewittjones.com/.
2. Hill, Napoleon. *Think and Grow Rich*. Wilder Publications, 2018.

CHAPTER 10

High-Performing Groups and Teams

It was a Friday night in 2017. I was on a Delta flight from New York to San Diego, where I took advantage of satellite TV to watch the women's college basketball semifinal games in Dallas. I was especially interested in the second game, between Mississippi State and the University of Connecticut. As I mentioned earlier, UConn was riding a winning streak of 111 consecutive games, being followed on a daily basis by an HBO film crew, and standing at the doorstep of winning its fifth straight national title.

While I enjoyed the streak as much as any UConn fan, I was far more impressed by the team culture that makes such a streak possible. This is a culture that doesn't measure itself against its opponents as much as set its own standard of excellence, one that inspires a relentless commitment to getting better each and every day. I'm not sure when it started, but the hashtag #AndCounting took on a life of its own once UConn broke its own record (ninety) for consecutive NCAA basketball wins (men or women). With each win thereafter, the number was always noted: 100 #AndCounting …

The prevailing thinking across the country, and especially for UConn fans, was that this team showed no signs of losing, and if they didn't lose this year, everything pointed to the team being even better the following year. ESPN's Kara Lawson speculated that 200 consecutive wins wasn't out of the question. But, as Head Coach Geno Auriemma warned time and time again, all streaks come to an end. Unfortunately for UConn, theirs ended that Friday night with a buzzer beater in overtime.

The winning streak and the program's eleven national championships are great headlines, but they aren't the story. The story and the lessons the coaching staff and these young women have to teach us lie in the team's culture. The streak that I believe matters most to the coaching staff, and should matter most to the players, is the number of consecutive days they add to perpetuating a winning culture and honoring the players who came before them. In fairness, during many interviews I watched throughout the season, the players talked about this quite a bit. They don't focus on the result; they focus on what makes the result possible.

To that end, I've created a new UConn streak, one that I regard as even more impressive than the number of wins. Let's call it the UConn "culture streak." I'll mark its beginning as January 31, 1990, the day the UConn women's basketball team played its first game at the new Gampel Pavilion on campus. The following year, the team would advance to its first Final Four, and in 1995, it would go on to win its first national championship.

The rest is history. As of today, its "culture streak" is more than 10,000 days #AndCounting.

What Our Guests Had to Say About High-Performing Groups and Teams

Life coach Simon Alexander Ong explains his views on the difference between looking at success as a destination versus a never-ending journey:

> I was giving a talk just last night here in London, and someone said, "How about people who consider themselves successful? What happens if you're already a success?" And I said, "Well, here's the thing. If you consider success to be a destination, the problem is, you're gonna fail very quickly." And here's the reason: What comes after success? When people get success, when they've think they've hit that destination, and they enjoy the rewards of success but forget how they got there.
>
> And that's often why, in America or whatever country around the world, it's a lot easier for a sports team to win that championship the first time—but it's a hell of a lot tougher to win it a second or third or fourth or fifth time. Because so many people focus on the outcome. But it's better to focus on the process, the journey, the everyday things we can do so that we always remain students in that way.

Jeff Hoffman, former CEO of Priceline and partner/co-founder of Colorjar, shared his leadership perspective on the power of letting go:

> As we all know, it gets harder and harder as you get bigger to find the superstars because, statistically, eventually you've hired all the A+ people. You've got to allow people to split into their own empowered teams and let them go, to let people take their piece of the business and own it and be accountable, which means letting go. They might

actually make a mistake. And here's a crazy thing: they might do it differently than you would do it, which will drive you crazy until you find out their idea was actually better than the way that you were doing it. You have to be willing to step back and let go and let people grow and be empowered.

That's the first part, which a lot of people have a hard time doing. There's an old saying that if you want something done right, do it yourself. Remember that? That is the worst possible advice you could give an entrepreneur who wants to scale, because the only way you're going to scale is to start letting go and letting more people take pieces on their own. You can't keep doing everything yourself because you think you know the best way. And when the team makes a mistake and they find out it's not the end of the world, and you say, "Hey, look, at least you're moving forward and growing," they'll start to get braver. They'll start to follow their instincts, and they'll start to realize you're actually trusting them to run their part of the business. Amazing things happen when people feel empowered to do that.

The other piece is making sure the teams know what you care about. Here's another story, which just sort of happened on the fly: We had a customer who was having a problem with our product. The account manager in our company assigned to that customer was having trouble solving it. The woman who sat over at the next desk was overhearing the conversation, even though it's not her client. When that account manager, who had a frustrating day because he couldn't fix the client's problem, went home, she picked up the phone, called that client, and said, "Look, everyone's gone. It's after hours, but explain to me again what's going on." She apparently stayed the whole night, and she finally went home at like, 5:00 am, and slept a couple hours. She solved the problem, which wasn't even her problem. She's not graded on it, she's not paid for it. She just did the right thing. She came up with a brilliant idea to fix the problem because no one else could solve it.

I overheard the story when I came in the next morning. Everyone was saying, "Did you hear what Natalie did last night?" I jumped in the car and went down the street. I had seen this sports trophy place. I went in there—this is all on the fly—and for twelve bucks, I bought a gold-colored martial arts trophy.

I walked in the office, and I stopped everybody. I said, "Everybody, stop working and stand up. Come into the hall." We call these our hallway standup meetings. I'm standing in front of Natalie, and I said, "Folks, last night, Natalie did something amazing. She stayed all night, solved a problem, and came up with a brilliant solution that you all need to know if your customer has this problem." I said, "For that incredible above and beyond the call of duty effort—and that is what I value, attitude and effort and going beyond—today, I am awarding Natalie with the first-ever golden ninja award for being a nighttime ninja and stealthily fixing a problem." I put that trophy on her desk.

Everybody was practically drooling over it. It was a $12 piece of plastic. They said, "How do we get that?" I said, "Just do something amazing." When I hear about the next amazingly innovative thing, about somebody going above and beyond, I'll award the trophy to that person. I said, "I'll tell you what, guys. The trophy stays on Natalie's desk until one of you takes it from her."

This $12 golden ninja statue became very desired. People realized it was a big deal, whoever's desk it was on. People wanted to impress management and do something innovative for that $12 statue, because they recognized that it represented the respect of the ownership, the management, and all of their peers. If it's on your desk, you earned it. We changed the process so the whole company had to vote and approve it. When you got that thing, you earned that thing.

It was a sweet deal. Making sure the team knows what you value is critical. What matters at this company? It gets them really motivated when they know they are achieving the things that make the company successful.

Some of the best respect you ever get is from your peers. Technically, they're also your competitors. You're all competing for the next promotion, job, et cetera. When your peers say, "Wow, you're doing great," for most people that's really hard respect to earn. It means a lot to people. I didn't overhear Natalie saying I gave her an award, I heard her saying that all of the people in the office came by to congratulate her, and that meant so much to her that the people she worked side by side with thought she did great. That's when I said, "You know what, guys, from now on, it's a group thing. You guys elect the next person." It was meaningful to people.

What Business Needs to Focus On

Rich Karlgaard, *Forbes* publisher and futurist, sees peer-to-peer coaching as essential to organizations of the future:

I gave a speech to Walmart's top 500 managers in September in Bentonville, and one of the senior managers told me afterward that they're very worried about competitors leveraging technology, like Amazon and Alibaba. Remember, Walmart was the company that disrupted Kmart and Sears back in the day, and now they are under threat of being disrupted. This guy said, "We think we're pretty good about technology, it's the culture that causes us to be too slow." Every conference call has thirty people on it. How do you develop a culture where teams can arise spontaneously at just the right size with just the right mix of intuitive thinkers and analytical thinkers, introverts and extroverts, men and women, people of various talents to most perfectly solve the problem or chase the opportunity?

You have to have a company where everybody understands what the company's mission is and people have not only respect and admiration for each other, they have almost a love for each other. You have to have a level of trust that your competitors or the disrupters can't take away. I believe a real driver of that culture is this peer-to-peer support, whether it's within a company or via outside peer groups. In many cases, the founder, the CEO of a 100-person company or a 50-person company or a 500-person company, feels all alone, feels the burden of being the head person in charge. That CEO often doesn't feel like it's quite right to wear their heart on their sleeves because it might scare people, the employees or customers or vendors. People are human beings. You might go through a bad patch with your children or your spouse or your health or simply a bad patch in your business.

Who are the peers within your company, especially if it's a small company? I think, almost by definition, that peers at that level have to be outside your company, and most of us can't afford a six-figure coach. Anyway, I think getting your coaching from peers is even more valuable because you get an honest discussion. Peer groups and workshops and such are absolutely the work that the world needs right now—and can this kind of support can really accelerate the personal evolution of the leadership at these kinds of companies.

Key Takeaways

Imagine a purposeful team whose members are committed to one another and who do whatever it takes each and every day to set its own standard of excellence. High-performing groups are made up of people who trust one another, who value being productive, whose word is their currency, and who enjoy a leader who believes he or she is there to make the team successful, not the other way around. The people on the team matter a great deal. It's time to develop a people plan for yourself and your organization.

CHAPTER 11

Crafting a People Plan

During my conversation with Claude Silver, Chief Heart Officer (CHO) at VaynerMedia, I shared a story with her about one of the things I did right—though I also made many mistakes—when I started Bottary & Partners. I felt compelled to share the following story with Silver because of VaynerMedia's commitment to its people, something I suggest is more the exception than the rule. At VaynerMedia, the CHO—not the COO or CFO—is the number-two person in the organization. Here's what I told Silver: Before I get into what commitment to your employees looks like in your company, I want to draw a parallel with a book that was very important to me when I started my small public relations firm back in 1995. I was both influenced by and enamored with *The Customer Comes Second* by Hal Rosenbluth and Diane McFerrin Peters.[1] I was so enthralled with the book, I remember writing to Hal Rosenbluth himself once I started my company, saying, "I want to use the 'employees first, clients second' principles you talk about in this book to build my organization."

It wasn't because I was trying to be a nice guy; I really saw the practical aspects of how the principles outlined in the book could help build and grow our business. The thing is, though, I remember reading the introduction and thinking, "Fine, the customer comes second, so of course your employees come first because they're the ones delivering the amazing service you want delivered to your customers or clients. Okay, I get it. So what's in the rest of the book? What could it possibly be about?"

In talking to Silver, I wanted to learn what the "employees first" philosophy looks like inside VaynerMedia. As Chief Heart Officer, she's number two in the company. So, in the same way Rosenbluth described in his book, I asked her to give a sense of what a real people-centric organization looks and feels like. Here's how she responded:

> I'm going to jump right in and tell you that our organization looks like a heck of a lot of collaboration. We sit in open offices, so we're dialoguing constantly with our teams, with the pods that we sit on, with people. There's a real camaraderie here. My belief is that our employees want to turn each other into champions. I firmly believe that. We come from a culture of we, not I, which is really, really important.
>
> Putting people first obviously means that I am spending all of my time with people. In one-on-ones, in town halls, I'm doing coaching sessions on helping people find their purpose, removing road blocks, dealing with grief, dealing with anxiety, dealing with people, with

life on life's terms. Gary [Vaynerchuk] is as well, and we have, well, "open door policy" doesn't even describe it, quite frankly. The door is flung open. The phone is on 24/7. We care. And because that came down from Gary eight-and-a-half years ago ... He created the culture. We were going to be a culture where we put people first.

My job now is to make sure the soil, the flower bed, is getting its nutrients. I see that people are getting the learning and development they need, that they are getting the conversations they desire. I'm understanding where growth and development work for them. I've got a wonderful team that works with me. They're HR generalists, if you will, and they're spending their time in one-on-ones or in small groups making sure that communication is flowing, that people are having conversations about what is going on with them. I really do believe that we are not only teaching digital social marketing skills and turning grad students into PhD students, we are teaching life skills here.

I have never, ever experienced an organization in twenty or twenty-five years of working where not only do we put people first but we care. We want to connect. We want to build trust. We want to feel each other. We want to be empathetic. We're human beings, and we are all wired to belong. Connection plus trust plus empathy and kindness equal amazing things. Amazing things happen. I hope I've given you a flavor of what our culture looks like. It's a very friendly, warm place.

Having a Philosophy Is Only a Start

What I learned from Hal Rosenbluth and Diane McFerrin Peters, from my own experience leading Bottary & Partners, and from Claude Silver at VaynerMedia is that it's one thing to have a mindset in which the client comes second and employees first, and it's quite another to watch the extent to which certain companies put that philosophy into practice. In *The Customer Comes Second*,[1] I was blown away by the authors' description of the way their concept worked on a day-to-day basis, just as I was knocked out when Claude Silver painted her picture of VaynerMedia's culture.

In my case, my employee-first philosophy was put to the test early, when I had a senior management-level client verbally abuse a junior account person on our team. The client ended the call with her by saying he would have her fired. She came to me immediately and told me what happened. The incident wasn't her fault at all. She just happened to be the person at the other end of this client's misplaced rage. I thanked her for letting me know what happened and told her that I would take it from here. I'm sure you can guess what I did. I called the client and fired him, making it crystal clear that he would never treat one of my employees that way again because he would never have the chance. I told him I would personally oversee the transition to a new agency, but that he was out.

For my team, that was a seminal moment. Does the employee come first when it could cost the agency a client? When it could cost the firm real money? The answer is, of course. The reality, however, is that firing that client didn't cost us a dime. By staying true to our values, we benefited in every way you can imagine, both culturally and financially. My employees realized how serious I was about Hal Rosenbluth's approach. It rallied the team, and they took it upon themselves to replace that client and the income associated with it (and then some) in what appeared to be the blink of an eye. We picked our clients as they picked us—carefully. My friend Reid Carr, who leads Red Door Interactive in San Diego, sums up his "philosophy" even more succinctly. He leads a "jerk free" workplace! Wish I'd thought of that.

Putting Ideas into Practice

While I've enjoyed tapping into the experiences and insights of some very successful people, and sharing ideas and stories, I'd be remiss if I didn't lay out a way to take this information and make it work for you in practice—both in life and in business. To that end, you'll find two *People Plans*, one geared for individuals and the other for groups and teams. If you're wondering why the individual plan isn't called a *Person Plan*, it's because that would imply it is a solo pursuit. It's not, and it never is.

I've taken Peter Fuller's advice about the power of three. Each plan includes three segments (Preparing/Planning/Playing) with three parts to each segment. You're probably noticing a lot of P words. Peter believes in threes, and I'm a sucker for alliteration. I figure if I combine the two, these plans can't miss!

People Plan (Individual)

My dad left the Boston Police Department in his late thirties and began studying and preparing to sell insurance. After winning a golf match with a buddy, my dad went to dinner with his friend to celebrate. My father had just turned forty, and this friend happened to be a golf pro. He turned to my dad at dinner and said, "What are you going to sell insurance for? Why don't you get into the golf business with me?" "Getting into the golf business" would require my dad to go to a school (run by the Professional Golfers' Association (PGA)), take all the courses, and pass the playability test. That is what it would take for him to earn his Class A PGA card. It's something most people pursue in their twenties, not their forties.

Four years and a lot of hard work later, my dad received his PGA Class A card and taught golf for more than thirty years before eventually retiring. Besides pursuing a career most people would have assumed had passed him by, my dad surrounded himself with the right people and did what was necessary to achieve his goal. He simply wouldn't be denied, and the people around him wouldn't have had it any other way. Knowing what my father went through to realize his dream, I can say unequivocally that this success was predicated on following every one of the steps outlined in this People Plan. He became a Class A PGA pro at forty-four—consider that fuel for realizing your own dreams. Here are the three segments and nine steps:

Prepare

- *Share*: Find someone, even if it's one person, whom you trust, and talk about what you want out of life. Let that person help you explore and discover what you *do* want, not just what you *don't* want.
- *Identify a specific goal*: Turn your dreams into specific goals. You can start small if you like, but set a goal for yourself that means something to you and make the decision to go after it.
- *Build your dream team*: Identify people who can help you achieve your goal. If they share the same aspiration, consider going after it together. Find people who've already achieved the goal, and get tips from them that will help you develop your own action plan. Enlist people who will encourage you and challenge you, and who will not let you fail.

Plan

- *Create a plan*: Use the input from your dream team to create your own action plan. Make it a plan that's realistic and plays to your strengths. Be as specific as you can about what it will take to be successful.
- *Stay curious/listen for understanding*: Just because you created a plan doesn't mean it's etched in stone. Be open minded, stay curious, and adjust your plan as needed.
- *Identify (and celebrate) small wins*: Focusing exclusively on the end goal can be psychologically debilitating. Identify near-term milestoness at the start of your plan and declare victory at each and every step along the way. Consider conducting a weekly call with one of your dream team members to celebrate your progress and talk about what's up for the week ahead.

Play

- *Leverage your dream team*: Whenever you and a dream team member can participate in a goal-achieving activity together, do it! Don't forget that you're not in this alone, and most importantly, have fun! This shouldn't be an exercise in drudgery. Make achieving your goal a team sport every step of the way.

- *Pay it forward*: Be part of someone else's dream team. There's nothing more satisfying than playing a part in another person's success. You'll find giving better than receiving in so many ways, and you'll create your own dream team culture of accountability.

- *Commit to continuous improvement*: The more you focus on what it takes to achieve the goal (rather than on the goal itself), the more likely you'll be successful. Remember the UConn women's basketball program? That team focuses on getting better every day—that's why they win national championships. The more you improve, the more you'll be equipped to achieve more of your goals more often.

People Plan (Team/Group)

The People Plan for Teams and Groups emerged from my workshops for business leaders, and is framed around the five factors common to high-performing groups and teams. I've marveled at the conversations group members have had with one another as well as those I've heard about from the CEOs and key executives who have facilitated similar exercises with teams at their own organizations. The workshop conducted for teams offers a forum for—and the permission to share—specific concerns as well as ideas that can make any team better.

Prepare

- *Have the right people*: Gather your team members, and ask them what attributes they believe are required of a person to make him or her uniquely successful in the team or organization. This can be eye opening. How many of us have been impressed with a resume and subsequent interview of a candidate, only to have him fail? This simple exercise can help you make such mistakes less often.

- *Identify a purpose/group norms*: Develop a collective understanding of the purpose of the team and its group norms. Why are you here, and how will you work together most effectively?
- *Create a forum for sharing*: Teams may work together, but they don't always know each other as well as you think. Assuming you have the right people with the right attributes, consider establishing internal peer groups where employees can share common aspirations and challenges and hold one other accountable for their own growth and success.

Plan

- *Build a trusting environment*: Sharing builds trust, but trust has many faces, including competence, reliability, commitment to the purpose, and so on. Consider trust a journey rather than a destination, and never take it for granted. A climate of trust is easier to build when your people see each other as people, not just fellow employees. The more they get to know one another personally and professionally, the greater the likelihood that they can establish a culture of trust.
- *Maximize productivity*: Having the right people who trust one another is a good start, but it doesn't guarantee high productivity. How can you be certain the team is firing on all cylinders? Start by asking your people how they like work meetings. Are meetings the bane of their existence, or are they a necessary part of being heard and staying connected?
- *Nurture a culture of mutual accountability*: Accountability to the leader is one thing, but the magic happens when employees feel accountable to one another. It's the difference between a good team and a great one.

Play

- *Identify and celebrate small wins*: Chasing lofty goals can be exhausting, and it can be easy for a team to lose focus if they can't see their progress. Map out interim points at which to declare victory, and celebrate often.

- *Practice servant leadership*: As a leader, you're there to serve the team, not the other way around. Be a good steward of the four factors—people, trust, productivity, and accountability—and everyone wins.
- *Commit to continuous improvement*: Invest your time and energy in continuous improvement. Pay attention to your dashboards, but don't obsess over them. Obsess over the activities required to make success possible.

An Exchange with Paul Michelman

As we consider developing and implementing our People Plans (individual or team), we need to be agile and adaptable. Paul Michelman, *MIT Sloan Management Review* Editor-in-Chief, shares his views on shaping our People Plans for the future:

> If we leap ahead, say, ten years, we start to see some core trends, and there are a few of them together; I'll walk through them. There are a few trends that we're seeing very much in evidence that are only going to accelerate and mature. One is that organizations are slowly but surely breaking apart, and many organizations that used to do everything, from soup to nuts, from the idea for a product through to its service over a lifetime, have found that they're much more effective if they concentrate only on the core.
>
> Without getting into the weeds of what that looks like, I really do believe we are accelerating—this may not be true for ten to twenty years, but change takes a long time—toward an era of networked enterprise, where organizations are smaller, they're shorter lived, people are moving between them much more quickly, and they are task oriented.
>
> A group of organizations will come together for a product or to solve a problem, and then they will disperse, and then they

will re-form with other organizations. If you believe even a part of that, you have to stop and question the traditional role of corporate culture. Corporate culture is meant to unify and to deliberately create a way for everyone to work together in a like-minded fashion. That's not what you want in the environment I just described.

In this new scenario, we have to move away from prizing alignment, which is a very traditional strength of corporate culture, and value instead the ability to realign. And that is exactly what I've described: the ability to form partnerships and then re-form them, both within an organization and between organizations. I don't see the traditional role of corporate culture having a great deal of value. In fact, you could argue it would be a drag on the kind of agility and facility we're going to be looking for.

Now, I believe that there are important cultural aspects to the world I'm describing. I think it tends to be more personal than it does organizational. I think it's more about what types of individuals are going to succeed and be comfortable in the environment that I'm describing. It's less about the organization, and it's more about the individual.

Key Takeaways

Creating a culture of success in today's fast-changing environment, then, is about the individual first, and then the organization. That's what the people plans in this chapter address. Work on yourself, help others work on themselves, and support teams in growing together. Do it by surrounding yourself with the right people. These people will ultimately help you do the things anyone can do more often. Prepare, Plan, and Play—it's that simple. Despite changes that threaten to redefine the role of humans in the workplace, the importance of humans in the world of work has never been more critical. As Angela Maiers would say, you matter, and since the world is depending on you, it's time to share your genius.

Reference

1. Rosenbluunth, Hal F., and Diane McFerrin Peters. *The Customer Comes Second*. New York: HarperBusiness, 2002.

CHAPTER 12

A Call to Action and Poetry

During my work as an adjunct professor for Seton Hall University, I had students write weekly reflections on what they'd learned and what they could have done better. It's a habit for me, even today. There's real power in taking a quiet moment at the end of every week to think about the past week. What did I learn? What could I have done better? What do I want to do more (or less) of next week?

Reflection

As you consider how you might use what you've read here in your own life, let's reflect on *What Anyone Can Do*.

First and foremost, consider Joe Henderson's assertion that, all too often, a person's success is not the result of superhuman feats. Instead, success is the outcome when a person does the things anyone can do—though most of us just won't.

One of those things anyone can do is surround themselves with people who can help them achieve what they want in life. When they find such solid supports, they tend to do the little things anyone can do far more often. They actually develop and practice the daily activities necessary for achieving success on a consistent basis—in other words, they keep putting one foot in front of the other each and every day until they get to the top of the mountain.

No person, including all my *Year of the Peer* podcast guests, ever became truly successful all on his or her own. All had help, and lots of it. They all had people by their side who encouraged them, provided advice, and helped them hold themselves accountable to their own aspirations.

In a world where trust in our institutions is low, we are far more inclined to look to one another for help, including following the prevailing sentiment of our peers on everything from buying a book or a car to finding the best college for our sons or daughters. We trust our peers, yet we can still do much better when it comes to listening and learning from others. The more we stay open to possibilities, new ideas, and people with whom we may disagree, the richer our lives can become.

In the 1985 film *The Sure Thing*,[1] Professor Tubb exclaimed, "Have some fun! Yes, sleep when you feel like it, not when you think you should. Eat food that is bad for you—at least once in a while. Have conversations with people whose clothes are not color coordinated."

Engage others in conversations where you can fearlessly express what you want out of life, no matter how lofty your aspirations. Find one person with whom you can talk and be open about what you want—and invite her to share her dreams with you as well. Be clear about what you want, not just what you don't want—and, once you come to that realization, know that you matter. Develop your unique gifts, and share them to benefit others. Imagine what the world would be like if we all realized how much we matter and acted on it.

When you know what you want, start looking for people who can help you make your dreams possible. Build your own dream team, one that includes a range of people who can help you develop and plan and stick to it, no matter what. Constantly assess who is on your team, and make sure you have what Rahfeal Gordon calls "a healthy circle."

When we set lofty goals for ourselves—such as my dad's decision at age forty to become a Class A PGA professional—they don't happen overnight. When you're focused constantly on a distant goal, sticking with your daily plan can be exhausting, which is why a lot of people quit. Set interim goals, take note of your progress, and give yourself as many opportunities as possible to declare victory along the way. It will give you and your dream team members the boost you need to achieve what you want, whatever that may be.

We learn better when we learn together, and the more often we ask questions for learning, the more opportunity we have to grow. We have easier access to people and information than at any time in human history—take advantage of it. Expanding your worldview will increase both the amazing possibilities available to you and your ability to help others.

Find your safe haven by either starting or joining at least one peer group. There's nothing quite like being in the presence of people who share common aspirations and in an environment that is free from judgment and where confidences are strictly kept. This is a place where you can be your true self, and your peers can do the same. It's where you realize you're not alone when it comes to your dreams, successes, or failures. It's profoundly liberating to be with a group of people where you don't have to put your best face forward 100% of the time.

As Lewis Schiff loves to say, "Good givers are great getters." There's a reward for generosity that can be even more gratifying than achieving our own goals. Anytime I've made even the smallest contribution to someone else's success, it's made my day. As others help you, pay it forward and help those for whom you can make a difference.

When it comes to the workplace or in the team sport we call life, being a good teammate and creating a culture of mutual accountability can be the difference between good and great, and success or failure. Looking at life in terms of abundance rather than as a zero-sum game will quickly lead you to the conclusion that we not only learn better when we learn together, we can accomplish more, too. In my workshops for CEOs, I ask them to pair off and thumb-wrestle one another. I tell them that the CEO who gets the most pins in thirty seconds will win a fictional $100,000. After thirty seconds is up, I ask each pair who got the most pins. Typically, I'll hear, three, four, four, thirty. So I say, "Wait a minute, how did you get thirty?" The CEO explains that one offered to let the other win as much as possible in the thirty-second time-frame, and they agreed to split the cash. Collaboration beats competition every time. That's not only true for thumb-wrestling. As you may recall, it worked for Litron Laboratories CEO Carol Tometsko, too.

High-performing groups and high-performing teams have five factors in common. To recap the five factors, they are having (1) the right people on the team; (2) a trusting environment; (3) a productive environment; (4) a culture of accountability; and (5) a servant leader who can serve as the steward for the other four factors.

Finally, because achieving excellence at anything is all about implementation and execution, develop your own People Plan—whether it's for yourself or your organization. The nine-step framework, which is divided into three segments, is detailed for you in the previous chapter.

What's Next and Why People Plans Will Matter More Than Ever

I asked several of my *Year of the Peer* podcast guests to share their views about the future and what will be required of us as we strive to meet the challenges of our rapidly changing world.

Vitaly Golomb, who leads global investments at HP Tech Ventures, offers a glimpse at what we can expect:

The future is a little scary because the difference in intelligence between humans and some of the lower primates is not that big, relatively. Primates might be around, I don't know, 50 IQ. We're about 100 IQ, on average, right? Super intelligence [artificial intelligence] will take off from 100 IQ and go to a 100,000 IQ very, very quickly. We are essentially going to be insects in comparison. There are all sorts of ramifications. Is this going to end civilization? Is this intelligence going to eliminate humans?

We'll leave that for a different discussion, but what's interesting and more on topic, I think, is the question of how we should be educating ourselves given this scenario. I have kids who are six and eight, about to turn nine. My question is, should they be sitting there in classrooms memorizing data like we were taught? What can they learn that they will be better at than AI when they graduate from school and start building a career?

I keep coming back to soft skills and to becoming more human. Empathy, knowing where to find information, creativity—these are all things that I'm trying to teach my kids proactively as much as I can, and keep them more human. I think, what's a career that's more foolproof than another? Truck drivers are certainly going away in the next five years. We have autonomous trucks already being tested. That's the single biggest employment category in the US. That's kind of scary from a political and economic standpoint.

Forbes publisher and futurist Rich Karlgaard shared a story of how Berkley PhD Bill Joy sees the future:

Malcolm Gladwell had a chapter on how Bill Joy accumulated his 10,000 hours in computing at the University of Michigan Computer Center, got his PhD at Berkeley. He was the software guru at Sun and in the early nineties before the web—it was obvious as it is today, made possible by the web browser and I-band communications—when it was still pre-browser and narrow-band Bill Joy imagined that there would be a world where there would be all these smart devices, broadband communications, people communicating with each other. He said the result of that is that we had to stop thinking of our companies as the sum of all the people on our payroll and had to start thinking about our companies as part of the ecology of our industry.

Choose2Matter founder Angela Maiers shares what it will take to matter in the years ahead:

I was at a technology conference and was asked, "What's the next disruptive force on the web?" Humanity. It's always been the force. Technology's never changed lives in the world. Humans have done that. People do that, people who believe that the world wasn't created by anyone better or smarter or wiser or richer than they are and who step up every day to create the world they believe they deserve to live in. Try to find your tribe. Try not only to find people who think differently, those who push boundaries, but then start recruiting for your dream team. Start recruiting for people different from you who will challenge you, who will push you, who will make you not remain comfortable.

YPO CEO Scott Mordell offers a perspective on what's around the corner as informed by the organization's global membership:

We're going from this information space to this automation space that changes the way humans work and build and grow and can learn. We're not quite at the inflection point but we're right in the middle of it—so the question is what we do going forward. Things have changed so much; when I was in college and in graduate school, they were all teaching me about things I was supposed to pay attention to. Now we're in such an information-rich world that we have to be thinking about what to ignore because no human can process it all. What a switch in just one business career, that now the task is figuring out what to ignore, what's real and what's not.

We need to adapt faster than ever to a lot of technological change and redesign our business models because we're all getting disrupted. Most of us just don't know how, and given that, humility of spirit and humility of opportunity is really what's next.

As human beings, we still want the same things. We want to succeed in business, we want to be loved, and we want to have people we are close with and to feel we have an impact on them. We want to have meaningful careers and meaningful lives. A lot of the core needs are the same. And so the nature of the interactions among individuals as they experience that will naturally undergo some nuanced change, but right now for us the question is, how do we continue to provide a safe space, a safe haven where people can engage their vulnerabilities and their curiosities without judgment? We'll change our tactics as we go, but that's our platform charge. We'll do things a little bit differently, but we don't need to innovate and say, "You don't need trust anymore, what you really need is a chip in your head." That's not going to be the case. There are eight billion people on the planet, and that number is growing all the time—it's still all about the people. So we need to help the people interact with the people in a much better way.

The Poetic Voice of Sekou Andrews

I began this book with a quote from Sekou Andrews because I know no one who turns a phrase with greater eloquence and purpose. So it's only fitting that Sekou brings us home.

So, here we are. Me at my desk, you at yours. Surrounded by four walls. And all we want is a room with a view. All we too often get is a view of a room. A boardroom that has seen too much of us, a bed-room that has seen us too little. Hotel rooms and airport terminals that we navigate by heart. We are ...adults, now. And too busy ... and working ...and, "Uhhh, no, tired," ...and "can't talk" to each / other ...and "mustn't stop" for each / other. And we walk congested city streets, colliding into each / other ...without ever touching each / other or ever crossing each / other's border or pulling back each / other's curtains for we are certain that we already know all there is to know about each / other, and that is that, we are each ... "others."

You in your business, me in mine. And these walls that confine and this all-consuming grind. And this nameplate, this sign, this silo, this line. And this business card trying to be all that defines me. And if I ever forget its purpose, the front side of it reminds me: "You know the drill! Heeey, let's shake hands...Let's get together...Let's do lunch...Let's do coffee. Here's *my* need. Here's *your* role. Here's my card. Call me!"

So, I know. I know it might sound crazy. But what if / we just decided to do it differently today? What if / we all decided to acknowl-edge that the front of our cards merely talk TO someone, while the back is a platform for dialogue WITH someone? For tapping into the collective intelligence that makes our whole greater than the sum of our smarts?

There are communities with which we preemptively surround ourselves, simply because they will be strong enough to give us the needed strength when we are too weak to do so alone. And they are our colleagues and peers, our friends and family, our spouses and lov-ers and life partners who give us a soft place to land. A place to hang our capes and break from being Super Woman and Man. We don't always need it. But when we do... we SO do. It is these exchanges, found on the back of our cards, that remind us of the possibilities that we have in each other.

I know, it sounds crazy, but what if / this is the "us" that's embossed on the back of our business cards? And if we took a second to look closer, we'd find what's shared and who we are. I know, it sounds crazy, but / what if we didn't get so stuck on the front, so folks didn't get so stuck on our front. And we handed out "Here's what I care about" instead of "Here's what I want"? I know… I know… it sounds crazy. But what if we seize this chance to rediscover each other beyond the handshake and behind the card, to swap our visions and share our struggles and exchange our hearts?

See, for true collaboration, you don't have to get all touchy-feely. But you *do* have to touch and feel. We do have to process our issues and face what they reveal. We have to admit that this world is struggling beneath business as usual, in order for us to commit to finally moving forward to business as mutual. Through an ecosystem built on the backs of our cards / a community to better the truth of where we are / and then tether it to the truth of where we can be / by challenging like mentors, and caring like family.

Invitation

In closing, I invite you to listen to Sekou's poetic voice presentation. As wonderful as it is to read, remember Sekou is a master of the spoken word, so don't miss listening to Sekou deliver a more extended version of this piece by checking out the Sekou Andrews episode on my *Year of the Peer* podcast.

I also want to ask you to join me at WhatAnyoneCanDo.com, where I'll be posting content and providing an open forum where you can connect with people who can help you achieve what you want in life and who would also benefit from your participation. You're not alone. Who you surround yourself with matters, and so do you. I invite you to do what anyone can do and share your progress, your small wins, and your major victories. Enjoy.

Reference

1. Reiner, Rob (director). *The Sure Thing*. 1985.

*"On your last day on earth, the person you became
will meet the person you could have become."*

—Anonymous

Appendix

Interviews from *Year of the Peer* Podcast

Andrews, Sekou. "Sekou Andrews: Making the Whole Greater Than the Sum Of Our Smarts!" Interview. *Leo Bottary* (video blog), April 27, 2017. http://leobottary.com/2017/04/27/sekou-andrews-making-the-whole-greater-than-the-sum-of-our-smarts/.

Carrington, Peter. "Peter Carrington and Being All in the Same Boat." Interview. *Leo Bottary* (video blog), July 7, 2017. http://leobottary.com/2017/07/27/peter-carrington-and-being-all-in-the-same-boat/.

Darling-Hammond, Linda. "Linda Darling-Hammond: Learning How to Learn Together." Interview. *Leo Bottary* (video blog), March 16, 2017. http://leobottary.com/2017/03/16/linda-darling-hammond-learning-how-to-learn-together/.

Daskal, Lolly. "Lolly Daskal and the Leadership Gap." Interview. *Leo Bottary* (video blog), April 5, 2017. http://leobottary.com/2017/04/05/lolly-daskal-and-the-leadership-gap/.

Dias, Miguel. "Miguel Dias on Scaling Up Online." Interview. *Leo Bottary* (video blog), July 20, 2017. http://leobottary.com/2017/07/20/miguel-dias-on-scaling-up-online/.

Foland, Ryan. "Ryan Foland on Engaging Your Peers: Listen More, Talk Less!" Interview. *Leo Bottary* (video blog), May 18, 2017. http://leobottary.com/2017/05/18/ryan-foland-on-engaging-your-peers-listen-more-talk-less/.

Golomb, Vitaly. "Vitaly M. Golomb: *Year of The Peer* Podcast—Accelerated Startup." Interview. *Leo Bottary* (video blog), February 16, 2017. http://leobottary.com/2017/02/16/vitaly-m-golomb-year-of-the-peer-podcast-accelerated-startup/.

Goodrich, Laura. "Laura Goodrich: Work With Others and Get More Of What You Focus On." Interview. *Leo Bottary* (video blog), March 9, 2017. http://leobottary.com/2017/03/09/laura-goodrich/.

Gordon, Rahfeal. "Rahfeal Gordon: 'Your Location Is Not Your Destination.'" Interview. *Leo Bottary* (video blog), February 23, 2017. http://leobottary.com/2017/02/23/rahfeal-gordon-year-of-the-peer-podcast-season-1-episode-7/.

Hayzlett, Jeffrey. "Jeffrey Hayzlett on Paying It Forward." Interview. *Leo Bottary* (video blog), June 8, 2017. http://leobottary.com/2017/06/08/jeffrey-hayzlett-on-paying-it-forward/.

Hoffman, Dan. "Dan Hoffman: We Learn Better in Circles Than in Rows." Interview. *Leo Bottary* (video blog), November 9, 2017. http://leobottary.com/2017/11/09/dan-hoffman-we-learn-better-in-circles-than-in-rows/.

Hoffman, Jeff. "Jeff Hoffman Speaks to the Value of Real Conversations." Interview. *Leo Bottary* (video blog), October 26, 2017. http://leobottary.com/2017/10/26/jeff-hoffman-speaks-to-the-value-of-real-conversations/.

Kouzes, Jim. "Jim Kouzes: *Year of The Peer* Podcast:—Learning Leaders." Interview. *Leo Bottary* (video blog), February 9, 2017. http://leobottary.com/2017/02/09/jim-kouzes-year-of-the-peer-podcast-learning-leaders/.

Li, Charlene. "Charlene Li: *Year of The Peer* Podcast—Engaging Our Peers and Why It Matters." Interview. *Leo Bottary* (video blog), January 12, 2017. http://leobottary.com/2017/01/12/charlene-li-engaging-our-peers/.

Maiers, Angela. "Angela Maiers Talks About Owning Your Genius and Mattering." Interview. *Leo Bottary* (video blog), July 13, 2017. http://leobottary.com/2017/07/13/angela-maiers-talks-about-owning-your-genius-and-mattering/.

Martini, Christina L. "Christina L. Martini Speaks to the Power of Diverse Perspectives." Interview. *Leo Bottary* (video blog), June 15, 2017. http://leobottary.com/2017/06/15/christina-martini/.

Michelman, Paul. "Paul Michelman: Working Together In a Changing World." Interview. *Leo Bottary* (video blog), May 4, 2017. http://leobottary.com/2017/05/04/paul-michelman-working-together-in-a-changing-world/.

Mordell, Scott. "Scott Mordell Talks About the Value of Shared Experiences and Having a Safe Haven." Interview. *Leo Bottary* (video blog), June 22, 2017. http://leobottary.com/2017/06/22/scott-mordell-talks-about-the-value-of-a-safe-environment/.

Ong, Simon Alexander. "Simon Alexander Ong Makes The Definitive Case For Mastermind Groups." Interview. *Leo Bottary* (video blog), August 3, 2017. http://leobottary.com/2017/08/03/simon-alexander-ong-makes-the-case-for-mastermind-groups/.

Ramberg, JJ. "JJ Ramberg: *Year of the Peer* Podcast—The Intersection of Business and Journalism." Interview. *Leo Bottary* (video blog), February 2, 2017. http://leobottary.com/2017/02/02/jj-ramberg-year-of-the-peer-podcast-business-journalism/.

Reese, Sam. "Sam Reese On Making Better Decisions." Interview. *Leo Bottary* (video blog), October 19, 2017. http://leobottary.com/2017/10/19/sam-reese-on-making-better-decisions/.

Ries, Tonia. "Edelman's Tonia Ries Talks Trust." Interview. *Leo Bottary* (video blog), September 28, 2017. http://leobottary.com/2017/09/28/edelmans-tonia-ries-talks-trust/.

Robertson, Larry. "Larry Robertson on Community and Creativity." Interview. *Leo Bottary* (video blog), April 20, 2017. http://leobottary.com/2017/04/20/larry-robertson-on-community-and-creativity/.

Sanders, Tim. "Tim Sanders on the Power of Love!" Interview. *Leo Bottary* (video blog), July 6, 2017. http://leobottary.com/2017/07/06/tim-sanders-on-the-power-of-love/.

Sanderson, Trent. "Trent Sanderson On Life Lessons and Elite Athletes." Interview. *Leo Bottary* (video blog), August 24, 2017. http://leobottary.com/2017/08/24/trent-sanderson-on-life-lessons-and-elite-athletes/.

Schiff, Lewis. "Lewis Schiff: *Year of the Peer* Podcast—Good Givers Are Great Getters." Interview. *Leo Bottary* (video blog), January 26, 2017. http://leobottary.com/2017/01/26/lewis-schiff-year-of-the-peer-podcast-good-givers-are-great-getters/.

Seeley, Bri, and Thais Sky. "Bri Seeley and Thais Sky: Talk About Un-Networking!" Interview. *Leo Bottary* (video blog), March 30, 2017. http://leobottary.com/2017/03/30/bri-seeley-and-thais-sky-talk-about-un-networking/.

Shankman, Peter. "Peter Shankman Talks About Helping People." Interview. *Leo Bottary* (video blog), November 2, 2017. http://leobottary.com/2017/11/02/peter-shankman-talks-about-helping-people/.

Shapiro, Leon, and Leo Bottary. *Power of Peers: How the Company You Keep Drives Leadership, Growth, and Success.* London, UK: Routledge, 2016.

Silver, Claude. "Claude Silver on Scaling the Heart." Interview. *Leo Bottary* (video blog), August 10, 2017. http://leobottary.com/2017/08/10/claude-silver-on-scaling-the-heart/.

Solis, Brian. "Brian Solis on Peers, Customers, and Shared Experiences." Interview. *Leo Bottary* (video blog), September 21, 2017. http://leobottary.com/2017/09/21/brian-solis-on-peers-customers-and-shared-experiences/.

Wadors, Pat. "LinkedIn's Pat Wadors Talks About Finding the Right People." Interview. *Leo Bottary* (video blog), April 13, 2017. http://leobottary.com/2017/04/13/linkedins-pat-wadors-talks-about-finding-the-right-people/.

Wenger-Trayner, Beverly and Etienne. "Beverly & Etienne Wenger-Trayner: Inside Communities of Practice." Interview. *Leo Bottary* (video blog), March 2, 2017. http://leobottary.com/2017/03/02/beverly-etienne-wenger-trayner-inside-communities-of-practice/.

Index